CONFIDENCE CURES

Nishthaiv Nirogyam
The Art of Self-Wellness

CONFIDENCE CURES

Nishthaiv Nirogyam
The Art of Self-Wellness

Lt General S. B. Sehajpal | Mrs Kiran Sehajpal

Title: Confidence Cures (Nishthaiv Nirogyam): The Art of Self-Wellness
Authors: Lt General S. B. Sehajpal, Mrs Kiran Sehajpal

ISBN: 978-93-92209-26-0

Edition: 1 (Reprint 1)

Published by:
BluOne Ink LLP

Publisher's Address:
306, Tower-I, Assotech Business Cresterra, Plot No. 22, Sector 135, Noida.

Website: www.bluone.ink
Email: publisher@bluone.ink

Copyright © 2022 Lt General S. B. Sehajpal, Mrs Kiran Sehajpal
All Rights Reserved

Printed in India at Thomson Press (India) Ltd.

Contents

Acknowledgements	vi
Introduction	1

PART I: UNDERSTANDING WELLNESS

Man	7
Wellness	11
Physical Wellness	14
Mental Wellness	16
Pranic Wellness	26
Spiritual Wellness	31
Blissfulness and Godliness	35
God	37
Human Evolution and Wellness	41
Wellness Way of Life	47

PART II: PRACTISING WELLNESS

Watchfulness	57
Way to Physical Wellness	64
Wellness Exercises	66
Wellness Bath	94
Wellness Eating	107
Wellness Drinking	122
Wellness Biome	125
Wellness Pooping	128
Wellness Sleep	132
Wellness Talking	138
Way to Pranic Wellness	140
Wellness Breathing	142
Pranayama	145
Tibetan Rites	152
Way to Mental Wellness	161
Way to Spiritual Wellness	178
Way to Blissfulness	186
Way to Godliness and God	188
Wellness Death	190

A Note to the Reader	198
Readers' Review	200

ACKNOWLEDGEMENTS

I[1] wish to acknowledge the continuous presence of my late mother, Smt. Kamla Vati, during the period of writing. I imbibed the values of patience, perseverance and spiritual temper from her. I have included her words of wisdom that she shared with me in my formative years. My father, Shri Shanti Swaroop Sharma, made me courageous and hardy. He taught me how to articulate my thoughts and write them down, which has helped me pen this book.

God gave me the good fortune to look after my father-in-law, Shri Amar Nath Sharma, in the last seven years of his life. I learnt from him the qualities of retreat and renunciation. His death as well as the death of my parents, which I watched at very close quarters, gave me an intimate experience of life passing away. I have shared these experiences in the book.

Our daughters, Ms Shavee and Ms Ketaki, and our son-in-law, Mr Akshay, have read the drafts and made valuable suggestions to improve the contents. Major General V. K. Sinha, MS, VSM; Brigadier K. P. Anand, MD and Lieutenant Colonel P. K. Sangal, BE, VSM have given honest opinions that have helped shape the book.

---

[1] S. B. Sehajpal

Ms Bhagyashree, BPT, MPT (Neurology) deserves special thanks for making illustrations for the book without accepting even an honorarium. She is part of 'Social Substance', a global group managed by Dr Arun Bansal from Panjab University, Chandigarh.

Our dog, Czaro, has also contributed to the writing of this book. During her last days when she was in the process of fading away, a realization dawned on us as to how time had mellowed her down. She had become blind and deaf but still managed to navigate the house. She had reduced her intake of food, become calm and virtually prepared for the eventual departure. Her last phase of life taught us many lessons, which have been included in the book. One of these lessons is summed up in a line by the world-renowned Urdu poet, Mirza Ghalib:

> '... *shama har rang mein jalti hai sahar hone tak.*'

'The flame of life goes on burning till the dawn of awakening, despite all trials and tribulations of life.'

Lieutenant General S. B. Sehajpal
Mrs Kiran Sehajpal

*Dedicated
to our parents,
Shri Shanti Swaroop Sharma and Smt. Kamla Vati
Shri Amar Nath Sharma and Smt. Raj Rani
and our grandson, Kanishq*

INTRODUCTION

Confidence Cures: '*Nishthaiv Nirogyam*' is the motto of the Army Dental Corps, where I have served for 39 years. I joined as Lieutenant at the age of 22 and retired as Lieutenant General, a little short of 61 years. When I joined the Army Dental Corps, it did not have its own Military Symbols that could differentiate it from its mother corps, the Army Medical Corps. I had the privilege to be its Director General and Colonel Commandant for two years. During that period, nine Military Symbols were created to give a distinct identity to our corps. The above stated motto is one of them.

After retirement in the year 2011, my interests drifted from dental surgery to psychology, wellness, spirituality, philosophy and literature, which I have pursued since then and tried to inculcate the knowledge in our lifestyle. This book is our experience of what we have learnt in the last ten years. The precursor of this book dates to my sickness in 2007. I suddenly fell very ill, so much so that I had to be hospitalized, where I was diagnosed with high blood sugar, high blood pressure, extreme anxiety and insomnia. From leading a life without medicines, I ended up eating almost 10–12 tablets a day. My thoughts, emotions and inability to cope with the pressures of life had made me sick. I had lost faith in myself. It was indeed very shocking for me. Gradually, I gathered myself, regained confidence to manage the adversity, and in the process restored my competence to cure myself. That is how I could reduce my dependence on medicines.

In the year 2012 we visited Jindal Naturecure Institute in Bengaluru, where we had the first-hand experience of how natural, non-invasive and drugless therapies can keep a person healthy and maintain a state of wellness. Since then, we have been visiting this institute every two years to reinforce the practices learnt there, to refresh and rejuvenate ourselves. In the year 2018 we tested our physical stamina and mental strength by going to Kailash Mansarovar Yatra— the toughest, most life-threatening and adventurous excursion. We were the oldest in a group of 40. In those 10 days, we did not suffer from any health issues, not even a headache, even when, we crossed Dolma La, at a height of 19,800 feet. Though tiring, we could do it because of the 'wellness way of life' that we have been following all these years.

Three waves of COVID-19 in India triggered us to pen down our thoughts. We feel these will help people who want to stay fit but have access to very fragmented knowledge about wellness.

Competence increases confidence. This book is an effort to make every reader competent to confidently cure himself. It is a self-help book. All procedures discussed in it are non-invasive. Wellness is becoming a billion-dollar business with all kinds of fads, magic potions and foods. This industry has created job opportunities for many and has earned profits for the stakeholders, but it has become another expenditure and fetish for the rich and famous. The points to ponder upon are whether wellness is the preserve and privilege of a few elite? Do we need to spend a fortune to achieve wellness? Should we burn a hole in our pockets to be well? Can wellness be spoken in terms of plain language, devoid of all difficult medical and scientific jargon? This book is an attempt to make wellness a household priority without spending money on wellness shops, products, food fads, spas, gyms and still enjoy a life of wellness.

It is critical to mention here that wellness is both a science and an art. We wish to share the art of wellness, which can be practised by everyone. The information given in this book is based on common knowledge and ancient wisdom in the public domain. We do not intend to analyse, comment or pass judgment on what has been published on the subject. Our effort is to share relevant knowledge on the subject in simple language. We do not claim any superiority or expertise. We believe that the practices that helped us may help you all too. Neither of us has been unwell or admitted to a hospital for the last 14 years. God has also been very kind.

This book is not a treatise on treating diseases and discomforts. In fact, the human body has amazing healing capabilities. The 'wellness way of life' suggested by us utilizes this potential. It is aimed at preventing diseases, containing them within comfortable levels and reducing medical expenses. We advise judiciousness and pragmatism while following the contents of the book. Do not overdo anything. Stay in your comfort zone and explore the chapters gradually. Part I of the book is about understanding wellness, and Part II is about practising it. However, it is not a must to follow the book chapter wise. You can dip your feet in any chapter and enjoy the complete flavour. Make your own sequence. Nevertheless, we recommend that the chapter on watchfulness to develop observational skills be read first, time and again for reinforcement, till watchfulness becomes a habit.

Habits die hard. Consistency and regularity in following the information in this book is the key to wellness. The book needs to be read five times—first for an overview of the concept, second for developing your own insight towards wellness, third for practising and implementing the concept, fourth for refining and fifth for revalidation from time to time.

Transform yourself first and then transform others. Persuade yourself for wellness. As Buddha rightly said, '*Appo deepo bhav*', meaning 'Be your own light'.

'Man is a disease' — these are the opening remarks in Osho's book *Medication to Meditation*. The statement implies that humans are not at ease. Everyone appears to be agitated and unhappy. Had it not been so, then hundreds of years before Osho, Guru Nanak Dev ji would not have said, '*Nanak dukhiya sab sansar*,' meaning 'the whole world is suffering'. Thousands of years earlier than Guru Nanak Dev ji, Buddha too said, '*jeevan dukh*,' meaning 'life is suffering'. Similarly, the wars described in Mahabharata and Ramayana also exist as reminders of human suffering and unrest. Humans have, thus, never been at ease.

It is obvious that the way humans are, they will not be at peace. Is this how humanity will go on, or is there hope? What is it in the human experience that keeps them on an edge? Is there a lasting solution to tackle this uneasiness? To answer these questions, we need to understand man and wellness to pinpoint what makes man uneasy. What is it in man that becomes uneasy? Let us also analyse some fundamental themes—how much has evolution contributed to make man easy? What efforts have humans made to be at ease? Only then we can know what more needs to be done, and how to do it. Despite the pain and misery all around us, how many humans are really interested in wellness? If there is even one person and you are that one, then this book is for you.

We wish our readers all the wellness at all times.

PART I

UNDERSTANDING WELLNESS

MAN

Know yourself to heal yourself

The child in the womb does not do anything. There is no need. The heart is beating and the eyes are closed. The child is in his 'being'. The 'doing' starts with the first cry because the collapsed lungs open to fill up the air. The doing never stops till death. Once the child's eyes open to see the world outside, the focus continues to remain on the outside. Everyone around the child, including parents, teachers and society reinforce this focus on others. Even early childhood rhymes draw the child's attention outside. Every child is familiar with the lines written by Jane Taylor:
 '*Twinkle twinkle little star, how I wonder what you are?*
 Up above the world so high, like a diamond in the sky.'

The diamond in the sky is worth the wonder, no doubt, but a more precious diamond is hidden inside all of us and deserves an inquiry too. Instead of wondering about the distant star, if we become inquisitive about our interiority, then the rhyme will read:
 '*Twinkle twinkle little star, do we wonder what we are?*'

We do not! We may have an intellectual answer to it, but existentially we do not know what we are. Unless we reach that knowledge, we cannot understand and fully grasp the subject of wellness, because wellness is vast, vague, complex and complicated.

What am I?

This is a baffling question. It has been attempted by scientists as well as spiritualists, but a theoretical answer cannot give any practical experience. An actual understanding of our real selves continues to evade us, because this question never becomes a quest. It stays as an inquiry of a student, but rarely leads to the inquisitiveness of a seeker. Most of us do not make any effort to find our reality, because we get satisfied with a readymade answer. Hence, we do not undertake the journey to find our own answer. If you are curious to know about 'yourself' then you need to travel to the time of your making, the period of conception.

Body

It is obvious that there is a physical body, which is referred to as 'I'. This body has been given a name, but this name has little relevance apart from providing an identity. You could be named anything. Your body is a gift by your parents: one half of the cell (ovum) comes from the mother and the other half (sperm) from the father. The union of these half cells makes one cell. This is the seed of the human body. The cell starts dividing and multiplying to make an outer layer, called the skin and an inner layer, called the mucus membrane. In between these two layers is the middle layer housing bones, muscles, blood vessels, organs and all else that makes the body. The outer and inner layers are attached to each other at various openings in the body.

Ovum and sperm carry genes from the mother and father and combine to form the genetic material of the new body. The potential of these genes, with innate memory and predispositions, is passed on to the child. The inbuilt memory of the seed cell is transmitted to all the cells during multiplication. This memory is retained in the cells irrespective of their position, place and function in all the three layers. That is why when any cell in the body is in distress, the entire body experiences discomfort. When the taste buds respond well to the taste of the food, every cell enjoys the taste. A stimulus to any cell is shared by all the cells of the body. This connectivity, through intercellular communication, is the means by which wellness measures, like massage, acupressure, steam, exercises, etc., applied to any part of the body contribute to the well-being of the whole body.

Mind and Soul

The story of 'What am I?' starts with the body. But there is more to man than the body. There is the mind and soul. How do you acquire these? The answer is steeped in mythology. You need to travel to the time, before the body is conceived. You must visit the time of death. At the time of death, the body dies. The mind of that body does not die because it has many unfinished agendas which it must finish. So, it latches on to the soul and travels out of the body along with it. When the soul enters a new body, the old mind also enters it to make a new body-mind-soul complex. The desires, the imperfections, the predilections and all other potentials of the old mind occupy the new body. This old mind in the new body is called 'sanskara' (subconscious impressions). The experiences of all the past lives leave imprints on the mind and condition the future behaviour of the person in the new life. It is the baggage from the previous birth which one carries in the new birth. This gives a continuum to our existence in rebirth and reincarnation.

Prana

Soul can only enter a body which has vital energy or prana. The vital energy is transferred from one living being to another—from mother to child. Till today, it has not been transferred to the non-living by any means. Hence, the dead cannot be revived. It is only a mother's womb which lends the environment for this to happen.

The body is the visible part of 'I', the mind, soul and prana are its invisible parts. Without the invisible parts, the body is non-living. Likewise, without the body, the invisible parts cannot function. Thus, it can be said that the body is gross and visible, while the mind is subtle and indirectly visible through the body. However, prana and soul are always invisible. The body and mind can be studied by science. Prana has also been captured by advanced photography and demonstrated as aura. Till date, there has been no scientific demonstration of the soul. It can only be perceived, and that too only by the individual. Hence, it cannot be studied. It is the subjective part of the body. The body, mind and prana are its objective parts. Whether the soul is an activity of neurons in the brain, as postulated by scientists, or one that has always been there that can neither be created nor destroyed, as claimed by spiritualists, is debatable. But both agree about its existence.

Body, mind, prana and the soul together constitute 'what am I?' Thus, the 'I' exists in layers: the innermost layer is the soul, which is covered by the mental layer. Both are within the physical layer. Covering the physical layer is the layer of energy. Transcending all these is the layer of bliss. The 'I', thus exist in five layers, which intermingle. Only for the purpose of understanding, we have separated them as shown in Figure 1.

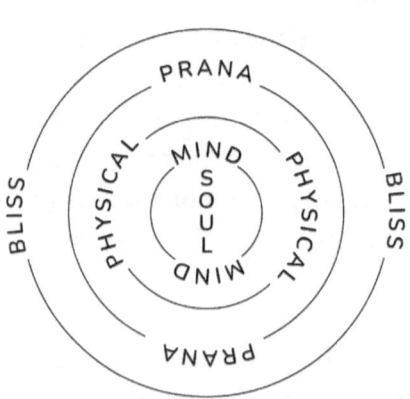

Figure 1. Schematic diagram of 'what am I'?

WELLNESS

Healthy is happy and happy is healthy

Although there are many scholarly definitions of the term 'wellness', yet the most apt one comes from the Sanskrit word *'videh'*, where *'vi'* means without and *'deh'* means body. Thus, *'videh'* means a state of existence as if you do not have a body. Wellness is a state where our attention is not drawn to our body and mind. Both body and mind are at ease. We do not suffer any discomfort. Acharya K. Lakshmana Sarma has summed up the standards of health in a Sanskrit shloka:

> *'Deh sarvatra chausnasya, samta laaghavam sukham,*
> *Kshutikshna, gadh nidra, ch manosoapi prasanta,*
> *Shareere karma samarthyam, analasya ch karmasu,*
> *Svata svedogama kale swasthya lakshayanti hee.'*

'The indicators of wellness are timely and effective movement of bowels, good appetite, deep sleep, sense of happiness, energy throughout the working time, optimum weight, clear skin, experiencing positive thoughts despite all odds and no pain in the body.'

Wellness is comfort, a balance, a midpoint between pleasure and pain. This makes wellness a very delicate state. Slightest deviation in body temperature, mild gas in abdomen, a little tenderness anywhere in the body, any disturbance in the mind or a change of weather can push the body towards unwellness. Since nobody can stay in the delicate state of wellness forever, there are bound to be periods of wellness as well as unwellness. If the period of wellness is longer, it is a state of ease. If the period of wellness is shorter, then it is a state of disease. It is important to recognize both these states to enhance wellness and reduce unwellness.

Why Wellness?

You can enjoy pleasure out of life and bear its adversity only if you are healthy. Wellness transforms one's physical appearance dramatically. It reduces the breakdown of the body, which minimises the need for food and artificial health products, medicines and other props. Wellness not only saves money but also creates a congenial atmosphere leading to manifold increase in creativity and productivity.

Wellness makes us happy. We are at our best behaviour of being civil and gentle with others. This brings a profound change in the social behaviour of others too. In fact, it has a multiplier effect in spreading good vibes, peace and tranquility all around.

Wellness is relevant from womb to tomb, and even beyond that. Wellness of the mother affects the foetus too. Wellness of parents is passed on to the children because they grow in an environment that promotes wellness. This makes them balanced adults who are sure and confident of themselves. A life lived in wellness prepares you to die peacefully. You may stay conscious and observe the transition of life from your body to beyond and get either a rebirth of your choice or freedom from rebirth.

Wellness of Layers

Wellness is comprehensive, but for the purpose of

understanding, it can be divided as per different layers of the body into physical wellness, mental wellness, pranic wellness, spiritual wellness and blissfulness. Beyond blissfulness is godliness.

Wellness of every layer is important. All the layers are interconnected because of which wellness percolates from the inner to the outer layers and vice versa. Wellness becomes more subtle as we proceed from the visible layers to the invisible ones. The more subtle a layer, the greater is its contribution to the overall wellness.

PHYSICAL WELLNESS

The body is as sacred as a temple

Physical wellness revolves around the functioning or physiology of the body.

Why Physical Wellness?

We are surrounded by diseases everywhere. Microorganisms are lurking in all nooks and corners. If we are not physically strong to counter their attack on our body, then sickness is inevitable. Physical wellness is, thus, the first line of defence. The physical body has senses which need to be satisfied, because only then one can think of wellness of other layers of the body. Mythology places great emphasis on the importance of the body. Both demons and demigods do not have a physical form. Demons have desires, which they cannot fulfil without the body. Demigods have no desires but need the body, the physical form, through which they bestow their benevolence upon those who need help. The physical body is so significant that both must enter a body to act out their intentions. While demons do not enter a healthy body, demigods do not enter a sick body. Physical wellness is of utmost importance because the physical layer contains and maintains the flame of mind, prana and soul. That is the reason the body is considered sacred.

How to Recognize Physical Wellness?

Your body has the necessary intelligence to give you a fair indication towards your state of health, provided you pay attention to it.

The body invites your attention to the state of uneasiness. It seeks your intervention to change the state lest it becomes a disease. It gives you an early warning to prevent and reverse the disease in its incipient stage.

You need to constantly watch your body to decipher its language, which is very subtle and innocuous. Some of the signs and symptoms of the onset of physical illness are lassitude or listlessness, fatigue, feverishness, altered appetite, a bitter or heavy taste on getting up in the morning, a coated tongue, dryness of the mouth, stiffness, aches, pains and tenderness in the body, swelling, foul smell of perspiration, too less or too much perspiration, dark coloured urine with a foul smell, dark, smelly and loose or dry consistency of stools, irregular evacuation of wastes and unnatural bleeding from any part.

The body also speaks in terms of feelings and emotions. Lethargy, loneliness and sadness may be experienced when the body is unwell. Happiness, joy, comfort, bliss, feeling alive and energetic are expressions of wellness.

There is a layman's way to judge the wellness of the body. *'Paer garam, paet naram aur matha thanda, hakim ke sar par maro danda,'* meaning that if your feet are warm, abdomen is soft and forehead is cool, you need not consult the doctor. You may have some discomfort, but certainly you are not ill.

Each morning, look at your face in the mirror carefully. Your eyes and expressions define whether you have woken up after a fulfilling night of sleep. If you have been restless in sleep, then you are unwell.

MENTAL WELLNESS

A calm mind keeps the body cool

Mental wellness revolves around the psychological aspect of your body. The human mind gives you the consciousness to experience the world, think and emote. Thoughts are fleeting in nature. They come and go in an endless stream. However, a thought that lingers on, moves into the deeper layers of the mind and becomes an emotion. Thus, emotions are spontaneous and do not result from your conscious effort. This state hovers around you all the time. It is like the weather surrounding you. It becomes a backdrop. Thoughts continue on this emotional screen and take the hue of the screen. That is why it becomes difficult to get out of the emotional turmoil. Thoughts and emotions are very subtle but very potent in their effect. Thus, an ounce of mental wellness is more significant in its contribution to overall wellness than a pound of physical wellness.

Mind

The mind is memory. Memory is the activity of the brain and gets stored in all the cells of the body because of which any disturbance in the mind affects every cell of the body. The mind is both individual, or personal as well as collective, or universal. Though it does not exist as separate entities, but for the purpose of understanding, we shall break it up, as shown in Figure 2.

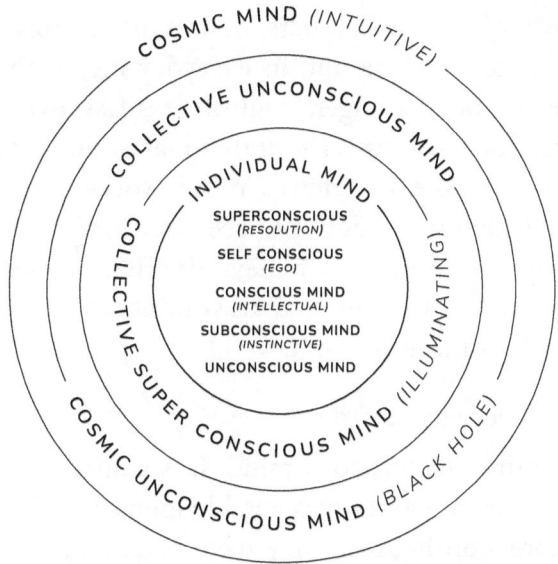

Figure 2. Schematic diagram of mind

Individual Mind

It is a storehouse of imprints, attachments and deep-seated mental tendencies carried over from all the previous lives. Individual mind defines every individual's personality. The individual mind has five layers:

Individual conscious mind

It includes thoughts, feelings and actions that an individual is aware of. It is a very small part of the mind, which is used for day-to-day living. It is rational and logical. Hence, it is also called the 'intellectual mind'. If mental turmoil is because of this mind, then one can become aware and act to reduce it.

Individual subconscious mind

It is below the conscious mind. It gives you conscience. It whispers to you from time to time. It processes the data that you accumulate and gives you instructions or solutions out of that data. It is illogical, irrational and is also termed as the 'instinctive mind'. The instincts, desires, obsessions, conflicts, fears and habits surface out, in everyday life, in the form of emotional outbursts, anger, anguish, restlessness and many other stressful reactions. The individual is not aware of the reason because the instinctive mind works autonomously. Your intellectual mind does not see your instinctive mind as the primary cause of your behaviour. Hence, you make no effort to eliminate the cause. With your effort, the intellectual mind may become aware of it.

Individual unconscious mind

It is below the subconscious mind. It is your individual past. It keeps unpleasant and unacceptable memories that have not found expression because they have been repressed by you. We may call it the 'personal dark mind'. It is the cause of your dreams, which allow you to purge the repressed. If that does not happen, a person is likely to experience some form of psychological distress.

Individual self-conscious mind

It is above the conscious mind. It makes you conscious of yourself and gives ego and attachments, which cloud your perception of the reality. We may call it the 'ego mind'.

Individual super conscious mind

It is above the ego mind. There is clear perception of your reality in this mind. The problems of the subconscious, unconscious and self conscious mind get resolved once you become aware of your individual super conscious mind. We may call it the 'resolution mind'. Instinctive mind and ego mind act as a veil, that does not allow you to reach your resolution mind. So, you do not get any clarity.

Collective Mind

It is the memory of all the creatures around you. It is common to all. It is vast and all pervasive. That is why the mind of every creature around you also affects you. The collective mind has four aspects:

Collective unconscious mind

It is made up of the unconscious mind of all creatures. It is the accumulated suppressed memory of the universe. It is the collective past. It contains past information of all the creatures from the start of evolution till date. It maintains this information without any prejudice or personal preference.

Cosmic unconscious mind

This is the primordial darkness from where the unstuck sound *'om'* and light originate. It is the 'dark mind' or the 'black hole' of the universe.

Collective super conscious mind

It is the mind of all the awakened individuals. It is also called the 'illuminating mind' because it is the mind of the enlightened ones.

Cosmic mind

It is the mind of God. It knows all. It is called *'prakriti'* in Hindi, where *'pra'* means prior and *'kriti'* means creation. It is the pre-creation stage. All creations are the product of this mind. God is above all these.

The individual unconscious mind or personal dark mind is your personal black hole, your dark side. It is dark because you do not let it come into the open. It stays dark till you visit it and let in a ray of light. The cosmic unconscious mind is the black hole of the galaxy. Every matter along with its information will someday return to this black hole. Earlier, science had maintained that nothing comes out of the black hole; whatever has gone in is destroyed forever. However, Stephen Hawking said that even black holes emit some sort of radiation. Matter that goes in gets destroyed, but it might be coming out in some other form.

During the discourse of Gita, Lord Krishna shows His *'viraat roop'* (enlarged form) to Arjuna to stress upon him that all beings must return to non-existence and then come out afresh in another form. It is symbolic of the black hole and *'prakriti'*. It may be inferred that the collective unconscious mind is the precursor to the cosmic mind, and that is how the cosmic mind knows all the past. It also knows the future of everyone because the new form comes out with new inputs given by the cosmic mind. Those who can read the cosmic mind can tell the past and even about the future. That is why the cosmic mind is called the 'intuitive mind'.

When the individual mind is in a state of turmoil, it cannot access the collective mind. So, it cannot grasp the actual reality which is different from your perception. Hence, the mental turmoil continues. Unless the individual mind is cleaned out, one can neither be mentally relaxed nor be receptive to the higher experiences of life for settling the cause of mental turmoil.

Nature of Individual Mind

It is the nature of your mind to become your master. It does this so surreptitiously that you do not even come to know of it. How does the mind become the master?

Strengths of the Mind

Mind is invisible. It shoots at you from the dark recesses which are difficult to identify. It is cunning and can deceive you by making you believe that it is not the cause of your problems but something else is. It gives you ego that does not let you accept that you are at fault. The mind is very sensitive. It can get hurt very easily and can make barriers around itself to dull its sensitivity. Therefore, all approaches to your mind must be subtle and delicate. The more you enforce, the more it rebels.

The mind is always active. It loves to move between opposites. It can shift to anything in no time. The mind is a hoarder. It accumulates each and every moment of your life forever till you ask it to unburden.

Shortcomings of the Mind

An understanding of your mind's shortcomings can give you a window through which you can override the strengths of the mind and become its master.

The mind can focus only on one object at a time. If you focus it on a neutral activity like breathing or listening to the heartbeat, it lets go off the other activity.

The mind gets fully absorbed in any activity or sleep, but as soon as the activity ceases or you wake up, your mind returns to its original state. Your mind has a default setting, but it can be altered.

The mind can be observed. The soul can observe the mind. A dialogue between the two can change the mental perspective from negative to positive.

The mind is never in the present. If you drop your yesterdays and tomorrows, your mind will cease.

Who Makes the Mind?

You make the mind, and then the mind makes you. You memorise everything knowingly or unknowingly. You do not let go of anything that is happening to you. You do not remove anything that has been stored. Since you make your mind, only you have the power to unlearn the unhealthy beliefs and not make it again. If you do not make your individual mind, then the collective mind around you has no effect on you.

Mental Turmoil

Three things need to be understood to get to the genesis of mental turmoil.

Purpose of Life

The basic purpose of life is to continue life. The creation which has created us must go on. Living beings have an innate urge and system to procreate and reproduce. Nature ensures that creation goes on whether you are willingly participating or participating by chance. The other purpose is to love, so that you can fulfil the basic purpose with the least mental turmoil.

Role of Life

Everybody values one's creation and makes efforts to keep it safe. These efforts unfold the play of life. You assume various roles in this play, at home and at work. This play is full of polarities, which give you contrasts and comparisons. You experience success and failure. You go through conflicts, competing desires, fears, phobias and shocks. You get complexes, conditioning, dogmas and fixed concepts. All these cause mental turmoil, which make the roles of life taxing. Hence, you need to love your roles because love dilutes the effects of mental turmoil.

While the roles recede with time, life continues. You feel a void or being of no use anymore. You cover up the emptiness by indulging in all kinds of activities, so that you can create more roles for yourself. You take up hobbies and vocations to stay busy. You become workaholics and keep yourself occupied all the time. You get caught up in the rut. But as and when you are alone this emptiness becomes evident. Emptiness gives mental turmoil. During this period, lot of people lament that there is no meaning of life. Rather than complaining, use this time to find the meaning of life.

Meaning of Life

You get so caught up with the everyday chores and activities of your roles that you either do not have the inclination or the time to discover the meaning of life. The ultimate meaning of life is to find your permanent entity, your soul, and use it to watch your mind and subdue it and understand the incredible relationship of this entity with the existence. If you do not persist to find this meaning of life, then you will not be able to detach yourself from the inevitable emptiness. This entity must be found by everyone on their own. A mere theoretical understanding will not do. Lack of this meaning of life is the biggest cause of mental turmoil.

How to Recognize Mental Turmoil?

Only an individual who can identify mental turmoil will try to surmount it. You can recognize your mental state with the following observations about yourself:

Are you Happy?

Ask yourself the question: Am I usually happy? If the honest answer is 'No', that means there is some mental turmoil. The more unhappiness and dissatisfaction you feel in your life, the more mental distress you will experience.

Can you Focus on the Task at Hand?

If you are easily distracted and it happens frequently, it is likely that something is weighing on your mind. A mind devoid of conflicts automatically focuses on the work at hand.

Do you Take Frequent Flights of Fancy?

If so, then you are daydreaming to escape from the present reality. It shows that you do not value what you have got and crave for what you don't have. This is one of the most underlying causes of mental distress.

Do you Sleep Well?

Observe your pattern of sleeping. Do you sleep soundly? Or are there frequent interruptions like twisting and turning while sleeping? Frequent disturbance in sleep indicates restlessness and distress.

What is Mental Wellness?

When the mind does not dictate you, when it does not make a slave of you but instead you have become the master, then you have achieved mental wellness.

Why Mental Wellness?

Mental turmoil keeps all the muscles tense. The continuous tension drains the energy from the body. Thus, the energy requirement of the body increases. So, all the systems of the body have to overwork to meet this requirement. This overwork causes inflammaging, which is the main cause of visceral fat. It is the fat that gets deposited around the abdominal organs deep inside your body. This fat interferes with the harmonious working of your organs. Gradually, the body weakens, its vitality goes down and eventually the diseases manifest in your body and mind. Mental wellness restores all the systems disturbed by unrest and revitalizes all the cells of the body.

A disturbed mind is not receptive to gather energy from the environment and food. If you stay preoccupied with mental problems, while eating, then you are not paying attention to your food. You are not enjoying the food. Absent-minded eating is usually hasty eating. There is insufficient mastication, digestion and metabolic activity. So, energy is not drawn properly from food.

While on one hand mental turmoil saps your energy, on the other hand it does not let the body replenish the energy. That is why it is stated that more than 70 per cent of diseases take their roots first in the mind, and later manifest through the body. Look for reasons of your unwellness first in your psychology and then in physiology. Unless the roots of a disease are removed, it will not go away, because psychology and physiology are interrelated. Calm and relaxed people suffer less illness than stressed people. The more you clean out the mind, the happier you become while interacting with the outside world. A person who is not happy will not allow anybody else to be happy either. The Sufi saint Kabir has concluded the importance of mental wellness as:

> 'Mann ke haare haar hai, mann ke jeete jeet.'

'Winning and losing is all in the mind; we give up first in the mind and then the body gives up too.'

Challenges to Mental Wellness

Humans are the only living beings who take themselves very seriously. They live in self-deception that their own mind is not the cause of mental turmoil. They struggle to control their mind because the mind operates through head centre as well as heart centre. The head centre is logical, but the heart is beyond logic. This complicates human psychology. Mental wellness is difficult but not impossible to attain.

PRANIC WELLNESS

Harness your energy for healthy living

Cosmic energy has existed since the time of creation. This energy can neither be created nor destroyed. It surrounds everything all the time. In fact, all matter is condensed energy. Energy is not only our source but also our saviour. According to the Sufi saint Kabir:

'Awwal allah nur upaya kudrat ke sab bande,
Ek nur te sab jag upjia, kaun bhale kaun mande.'

'First of all, God created light (energy) and then from it, nature created all the mortals. Since the entire universe has grown from one divine light, whom to call good or bad!'

Guru Nanak Dev ji has spoken the same eternal truth in another way: *'Ek pita, ekas ke hum barik,'* meaning 'there is only one father who is the source of all creation; we all are His children.' Ramanuj has expressed it in more detail in Saranagati Gadyam:

'Tvamev mata ch pita tvamev,
Tvamev bandhu ch sakha tvamev,
Tvamev vidya dravinam tvamev,
Tvamev sarvam mum dev dev.'

'You are the mother, and you are the father. You are my relative, my friend, the source of all true knowledge, and you are matter. You are everywhere, even in my demigods.'

This intuitive wisdom of the mystics has been supported by scientists too. They say there was only energy at the time of the Big Bang. Everything is a blob of the same energy. The saint and sinner are made of the same energy. At the quantum level, there is no difference between the living and non-living matter. This is an indubitable truth and a spiritually uplifting understanding of oneness. The differences that exist between us are man-made and artificial. If everyone starts to acknowledge this truth, then the conflicts of race and religion will cease to be. This will usher in everlasting peace.

What is Prana?

Prana is a Sanskrit word for the part of cosmic energy which one uses to stay alive. It is the essence of our existence, the vitality within us. Energy in space around the body is pranic body. It is an energy envelope in which the physical body, mind and soul are contained. It is also called ethereal body.

Kirlian photography has captured this envelope on a photo film. Scientifically, prana is termed as bioplasmic energy, which means energy around the living beings. This energy is not electrical, magnetic or thermal. It is bioluminescence (light). Semyon Kirlian was an Armenian researcher who demonstrated that while the bioluminescence of non-living beings has constant intensity, the bioluminescence goes on varying in living beings depending on the breathing and nutrition in the body. This photography also showed that the bioluminescence varies in a healthy and unhealthy person. It also demonstrated that bioluminescence leaves the body when one is dying. Kirlian demonstrated that blobs of energy get ejected out of the body till bioluminescence becomes static and the living being becomes non-living.

Breath and Prana

Breath is not prana. Breathing is an activity of the lungs. Prana is the flow of vital energy in the whole body. It flows by riding on the breath which gives us oxygen. Though breath and prana are not the same, yet they cannot be without one another.

Soul and Prana

Soul is not prana. Prana is energy. Soul is not energy. It is something beyond energy and defies description. The soul is passive and witnessing while prana is the active and non-witnessing part of existence. For life to exist, prana, soul and breath must be present. Prana is a vehicle or medium for the soul.

How Do We Get Prana?

Prana is passed from the mother to the foetus. It keeps the foetus alive in the womb. If there is no prana in the newborn, it cannot breathe at the time of birth. Prana in the newborn can continue only if the newborn breathes. That is why there is a tense moment for the newborn and the doctors till the child breathes. A newborn baby's lungs are all developed but are not used in the mother's womb. They become functional after the first inhalation, which is the first cry of the child. Prana is replenished by the energy from the environment through air, food, water, heat and light.

Why Pranic Wellness?

Prana is *'jeevan shakti'*, meaning 'life force'. It is the vital energy for a living being. Pranic wellness revolves around the capability of the body to gather and utilise vital energy for its physiological and psychological functions. When this vital energy returns to the source, the life of that body ends. Body, mind, prana and soul are in an intimate link. Disturbances of mind and body affect the pranic body and vice versa. However, the soul never gets disturbed.

Pranic Pathways

As per ancient philosophies which are intuitive rather than scientific, prana flows in well-defined pathways in the body as shown in Figure 3. These have been called *'nadis'* in Hindi, meaning 'channels' or pranic pathways. These are not nerves or blood vessels or any other physical structures. The pranic body receives energy from the surroundings. When physical body is healthy, the pathways allow smooth flow of prana. When physical body is unhealthy, it does not receive this energy properly and optimally. Any obstruction in the free flow of energy in these pathways makes the body and mind sick.

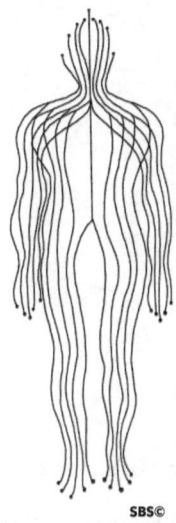

Figure 3. Pathways for the flow of prana.

Pranic Centres

The flow of energy in the pranic pathways is controlled by various centres called *'chakras'*, also known as vortices or pranic centres. These, too, are invisible like the pranic pathways. They spin and regulate the flow of vital energy. There are seven main vortices which correspond to the seven glands of the endocrine system. They regulate the hormonal output of the glands to maintain all the body functions. The first chakra is the *'muladhara chakra'*, centred on the reproductive glands, the second is the *'svadhisthana chakra'*, centred on the adrenal glands, the third is the *'manipura chakra'* centred on the pancreas, the fourth is the *'anahata chakra'* on the thymus gland, the fifth *'vishuddha chakra'* on the thyroid gland, the sixth *'agya chakra'* on the pineal gland and the seventh is the *'sahasrara chakra'*, centred on the pituitary gland, as shown in Figure 4.

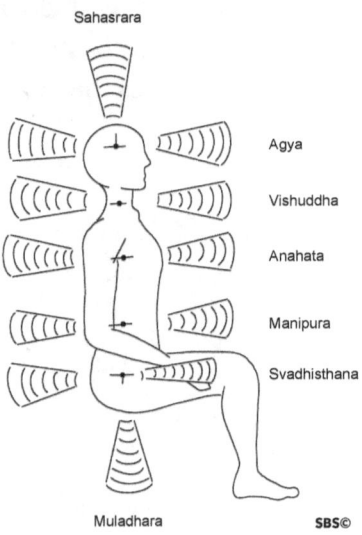

Figure 4. Position of pranic centres in the body.

The simultaneous spinning of these centres at optimal speed ensures wellness. When all vortices spin at the same rate, we are healthy. When these vortices slow down or spin at different speeds, we fall sick or grow old. When they are not in harmony, the slower ones and the faster ones cause deterioration in the related parts of the body. If we normalise the rate of speed of these vortices, the sick and old will become healthy and young again. This is the basis of pranic wellness.

Prana is even more subtle than mind. Pranic wellness is, thus, more consequential than physical and mental wellness.

SPIRITUAL WELLNESS

Silence is serenity

Spirit is the active principle of a substance without which that substance will lose its true nature. Soul is the spirit of living beings.

Soul

Soul is pure consciousness. It has no content. It is different from mind consciousness because mind has contents of thoughts and emotions. Soul is an eternal flame of life in every living being. It is eternal because it has neither been created nor can be destroyed. It is not made up of anything, hence is beyond senses and description. It cannot be deflected, obstructed, increased or decreased. The body and mind grow old, but your soul does not. It is there when you are a child and continues to remain even while your childhood goes away. It travels into the youth and then into the old age. The element which travels unaltered through different stages of life is your soul. It is the only constant. Rest everything else will change. The presence of the soul in you is the reason, that irrespective of your age, you can see that the child in you is still alive. The soul will witness the depletion of your strength in moments of pain, grief and depression, etc., but it per se remains the way it is. Without the soul, there can be no mind. Without the mind, there can be no intellect. Without the intellect, there can be no evolution. Thus, the soul is the foundation—the root and the basis of the continuum of life. The soul is still and silent. Ruskin Bond in his poem *'The Silent Birth'* concludes:

> *'...So must we search*
> *For the stillness within the tree*
> *The silence within the root.'*

The soul is a mystery, but it is knowable. It is within the individual and one can try to know it. Your search reveals your soul. Till one has searched and found, one has only acquired theoretical knowledge of one's soul. As George Gurdjieff, the Russian philosopher and mystic, once said, 'You do not have your soul till you have created it.'

Everything in the existence is interconnected and affects each other. The soul is that connector because it knows about everything. It knows all about you from the first birth onwards. It will know about you in the future too. The soul also knows about other things around it. That is why this layer of the body is called the layer of knowledge.

The soul observes in a passive, non-judgemental and unattached manner. It carries unaltered information about you, which has not been coloured by your mind; it is this information that can reach God.

What is Spirituality?

Soul is called *'atma'* in Sanskrit. Its source is called *'paramatma'*, which means the Supreme Soul or God. Spirituality is the connection of your soul with the Supreme Soul. It is a communication from pure consciousness (soul) to the source of pure consciousness. Spirituality is not religion. It is a step beyond religion.

What is Spiritual Wellness?

Spiritual wellness is an awakening that allows you to witness your core, the soul. The soul has always been there but as a passive observer. Spiritual wellness is a state in which the normally passive soul becomes an active watchman.

Why Spiritual Wellness?

The soul is higher than the body and mind. If you work on the higher levels, then the challenges posed to the lower levels will automatically be solved. This makes spiritual wellness the most significant. The soul is privy to that knowledge which cannot be known by your mind but is the cause of your unrest. Spiritual wellness is a stepping stone to that knowledge.

Active soul guides you to maintain your body, mind and prana. You create a peaceful environment for unleashing the optimum potential of your genes for your healing.

You become your own light to see the reality behind your identity and that of others. You do not see others different from you. This harmony helps in your wellness. Your ego drops. You are without your persona, your mask. Now your soul communicates with God. You can enter God's presence. You can experience godliness. This transforms the animal within you to the human and further to the divine. This transformation will travel with you to your next birth. Spiritual wellness is, thus, the key to unconditional happiness, enduring peace and bliss.

How to Recognize Spiritual Wellness?

Silence is the bloom of spiritual wellness. Silence is not due to the absence of everything. It is because of placid presence of everything. Nothing has changed but you have become silent.

Spiritual wellness gives you serenity. You accept yourself the way you are. So, no more competition and comparing because you are happy the way you are. Instead, you will be inclined to pull others out of their sufferings and miseries.

Lastly, if the word soul does not bring up your personal perception about your soul, then it is still a theoretical concept for you. You have not achieved spiritual wellness yet.

BLISSFULNESS AND GODLINESS

Wisdom is wealth

Blissfulness is a state of neutrality and equipoise, where both the negative as well as the positive cease to affect you. You are not influenced by the fluctuations and imperfections of time and circumstances. It is a state beyond your soul. Buddha has called it *'annata'* (no *atma*). You have entered the realm of the collective super conscious mind, the illuminating mind. Blissfulness is the ultimate state of wellness and ultimate quest of religion and science. It lends one an ageless body and a timeless mind. It is a prelude to gracefulness.

What are the Signs of Blissfulness?

A blissful person dwells in solitude. There is no dependence on anybody. You feel complete in yourself and are always full of gratitude for every situation and every person around you. There is abiding joy for no reason at all. You cannot pinpoint the reason for your joy. One experiences enstasy, the opposite of ecstasy. While ecstasy is an external expression of joy, enstasy is an internal expression of joy. You become quiet, calm, cool and collected. Your silence is not noiselessness, rather it speaks as peace and tranquillity. You are not imprisoned by divisions of race, religion, sect, caste, creed, colour or nationality. This makes you love everything and everyone, but such love is asexual.

True compassion is another quality of blissfulness. True compassion means when other person's needs override your personal needs. You give priority to others over yourself. As per ancient lore, when Buddha was in the process of leaving his body to enter into *'mahaparinirvan'* (the journey to a realm from where there is no return for a rebirth), he retreated behind a tree and asked his disciples not to disturb him as he was now preparing to go beyond. A villager who heard that Buddha was shedding his body came rushing, leaving all his chores aside, so he could have Buddha's blessings before he is gone forever. While he had been postponing meeting Buddha on some pretext or the other, he knew that if he missed seeing Buddha now, he would never ever see him. His arrival created a commotion because the monks would not allow anyone to disturb Buddha. But the man was firm and refused to go back without seeing Buddha. On hearing the commotion, Buddha said, 'My journey can wait, send him to me.' This is true compassion, because Buddha helped someone in need, even if that meant delaying the fulfilment of his own goal.

Godliness

Godliness is the end state. One experiences this state because of being blissful. It is a state where you connect with the cosmic mind. Though the mind can disturb even the most blissful person, but when you are blissful even in adversity, you are in a state of godliness.

When you dwell in a state of godliness, you become graceful without being aware of it. No human is born complete. Gracefulness completes a human. Gracefulness means an unruffled demeanour. It means to be smooth, relaxed and attractive. Godliness is the ultimate wellness. God is beyond godliness.

GOD

He is the be all and end all

God is the ultimate mystery and will stay a mystery because God is unknowable. He has been there even before the creation and will be there after it too. God is the creator. He is *'purush'* that brings creation out of *'prakriti'*, the cosmic mind or God's mind. *Purush* and *prakriti* come together to create. *Prakriti* is the womb, feminine element of creation. *Purush* is the initiator, the masculine part. That is why God is addressed as 'He'. God is the centre of the creation. He is within his creation and not external to it. He is not like a painter sitting outside the painting He is the dance in the dancer. Those of us who deny God cannot deny this existence, this world in which they are living.

Existence is not chaos. It is cosmos. As Albert Einstein said, 'God is not playing dice'. There is a system, a principle or some supreme entity that regulates this existence. Those who do not believe in God still believe in the principles running the cosmos. Lord Mahavira and Buddha have never spoken of God because they realized that He cannot be spoken about. But both the religions that they propounded believe in the soul and the system running the universe.

Whether God is there or not has never been settled. It will never get settled, because those who believe and those who do not believe want to prove themselves right by relying on logic. The supreme entity is beyond logic because it has never been known. Logic works with something that is known. As Eddington rightly said, 'The more I think of the world, the more I come to understand that the world is not a thing but a thought.' Einstein also said, 'The deeper I go into understanding the world, the more I realize that layers after layers continue to open. It is endless.' What Eddington and Einstein were saying was that there is always something more than what can be known. They are almost touching the realm of God to say that God is abstract and unknowable. What can be known is world. What can never be known is God.

There are questions, exclamations and statements about God, but no definite answer. The following verses say it in a nutshell:

'Kahin rahne ko tera makaan bhi hai?
Kahin milne ko tera nishaan bhi hai?
Tera charcha sab ki zubaanon pe hai.
Tera shor zamane ke kanon mein hai.
Tujhe dhunda to tu na mila, tera ghar na mila,
Tu dil mein to aata hai, par nazar nahin aata,
Shayad yahi teri pehchaan hai!'

'Do you have a dwelling? Do you have an identification mark? Everybody talks about you and that discussion has drowned the whole world in its din. I searched but could neither find you nor your abode. My heart can feel your presence, but my eyes cannot see your person. Perhaps that is the way you identify yourself.'

God is a presence and not a person. He can be felt but cannot be described. The Hindu understanding of God has two concepts: *'sagun'* and *'nirgun'*. *Sagun* means He has a form. His properties and attributes can be described. Idol worship is a result of this concept. *Nirgun* means He is formless. He cannot be described through any properties and attributes, hence cannot be made into an idol. Non idol worshippers follow this concept. Hindus accept both the aspects of God, and hence see Him in everything visible as well as invisible. That is how God is both *sagun* as well as *nirgun*. Therefore, He is also described as being '*sarv gun sampann*' meaning 'endowed with all attributes while also being without attributes'.

If you can feel His presence in a thing, then that thing becomes God for you. If you see His presence as life in living beings, then every living being is God for you. If you cannot see his presence in the living, then certainly you cannot see Him in the non-living. But even the non- living cannot exist without him. God is in sound as well as in silence. That is why He is complete and whole. Everything else that forms part of His creation must strive for completion, for wholeness. Evolution is a consequence of this perpetual strife to be whole.

Why is God unknowable? Firstly, God is not made of anything. Secondly, God has three aspects: the one that gives you birth is Brahma; the one that maintains you is Vishnu and the one that destroys you is Shiva. Our senses can perceive only one aspect or one dimension at a time, so the combination of the three, also known as '*trimurti*', is not perceived. Thirdly, God is in everything of the creation as its soul. One can know one's own soul, but only extrapolate or conjecture about the soul of another. This will be information and not knowing. God can be understood but cannot be seen, so He cannot be fathomed, and hence will stay unknown.

Soul is like the roots of a tree; the prana forms the stem; the body its branches; the mind is leaves, flowers and fruits; the fragrance of flowers and fruits is godliness and taste in fruits, or anything is God. You can perceive the fragrance, but you cannot see it. You must bite the fruit to taste it. Having tasted it, you cannot describe it in words. What you tasted cannot be known by those who have not eaten the fruit. Like taste, God is hidden in everything.

God is communicable. If that is not so, then whom do you look up to? Who answers your prayers and solves your problems? In the absence of God, you will feel hopeless and helpless—a situation not conducive to wellness. If there is no God, then we must create one to be hopeful. We can communicate with God because He is omnipresent as soul in everything. He is omniscient as the soul knows everything and is omnipotent as nothing is beyond Him.

Creation is an ongoing process. The creator must also be working to put humans at ease because all parents make the best efforts to keep their children comfortable. How evolution has made these efforts needs to be understood.

HUMAN EVOLUTION AND WELLNESS

Your past dictates the future

The life of earth is estimated to be around 10 billion years, half of which has already passed. It is impossible to predict the future of humans, but a careful study of the past may offer some answers to our existence in future.

Physical and Mental Evolution

Life began with a single cell organism and evolved into multicellular organisms over a long period of time. Gradually, the work centre, head centre and heart centre came into being, because of which the body and mind have been continuously evolving. The work centre supports physical development and gets activated only by physical work. It is located in the navel area. This centre is so sensitive that a forceful hit at it can prove fatal. The Japanese traditionally committed hara-kiri by piercing this centre with a sword for instant death. The head centre enables the development of mind. It is located in the head region. Thoughts, memories, instincts, intellect, coordination of all the body functions are controlled by the head centre. This centre functions on logic, because of which behaviour patterns of all living beings become individualistic and distinct from each other. It gets activated by thoughts and can be influenced by chemicals. The heart centre aids the development of feelings. It is located in the region of the heart. It is not the anatomical heart. This centre is activated by emotions and can be regulated by chemicals and suggestions from oneself or others. The heart centre knows no logic. It knows love, without which life has no meaning. This centre makes you understand the invisible soul and unknowable aspect of existence, which may be called God.

Problems arise from the head centre, but resolutions happen in the heart centre. The heart centre, thus, is the most significant. Sheikh Imam Baksh Nasikh, an Urdu poet, summed up his thoughts as follows:

'Zindagi zinda dili ka naam hai,
Murda dil khak jiya kartein hain!'

'Life is to be lived from the heart. Those whose hearts are dead, are dead indeed and their life has no meaning.' Thus, the ultimate wellness happens only in the heart.

Abraham Maslow, an American psychologist who attempted to understand human evolution, propounded the Hierarchy of Needs. It is a five-tier model of human needs, often depicted in the form of a pyramid.

Figure 5. Pyramid of needs

The survival needs like food, clothing and sex are placed at the base of the pyramid. After that is the need for safety and security. Once these two needs are met, one aspires for love and belonging. It is due to this need that we interact socially and build relationships with family and friends. Most humans do not go beyond this need. However, a small percentage is motivated and fulfils the need for self-esteem. This could include the need for accomplishment, working to build a prestige, to enhance one's sense of 'I am'; it is this need that motivates one to venture on a creative path.

Creativity does not always mean being a poet, sculptor, writer or an artist. It may be expressed in our everyday life, such as decorating the house, cooking a more appealing meal, grooming oneself, creating an atmosphere of love and affection, etc. This is followed by the need for self-actualization, which is placed at the top of the pyramid. This apex need is felt by very few people.

Self-actualization means to constantly strive towards improving oneself because there is always scope for improvement, but within one's potential which varies with everyone. A narrative from the Hindu epic, Ramayana is worth sharing here. One day, Lord Rama was praying to the Sun God in the forest. A curious onlooker approached him and asked, 'We all pray to you for our needs. But I see that you also pray to the Sun. What do you ask for?' Rama replied, 'I pray to the Sun to give me strength and wisdom, so that tomorrow, I can present to the Sun, a better Rama than today.' This is self-actualization. Irrespective of who you are, you can still improve. This is an astounding revelation. We all can make sincere efforts to become better humans.

Maslow also observed that, in general, unless the need lower in order is satisfied, the need higher in order of the pyramid is not even felt. Humans, with all their intelligence, have not been able to ensure that each of them fulfils the basic needs of survival, security and social interactions, so that they can think of being creative and attempt self-actualization.

However, Maslow was not a mystic. So, he could not think about self-realization, which is beyond self-actualization, and God-realization, which is beyond self-realization.

Evolution of Intellect

Stephen Hawking said, 'Intelligence is the ability to adapt to change.' Animals live by instinct, while human beings live by intellect. This is how evolution has made humans different from animals. While animals are limited in potential because of their instinct, intellect gives humans the limitless potential—to question, prevent suffering, be creative, adapt to changes, go beyond their animalistic instincts, become more humane, strive towards blissfulness and godliness. The unquenchable quest to know God gives endless potential to human evolution.

Awareness

Animals are aware of their surroundings, but they are not self-aware. Awareness of the self is peculiar to humans. Intellect gives you awareness about yourself. It also gives you the free will to choose if you would want to develop this awareness further or not. That is why not all humans are self-aware. Humans who live with awareness lead a more fruitful, creative and peaceful life. Sri Aurobindo has called these humans 'supramental'.

Freedom is the dignity evolution has bestowed on humans. Having given the highest mental faculties to human beings, nature has left it to them to evolve further and become comfortable. Whether we do that or not is a choice. Whether we do it collectively or individually is also a choice. It is possible that humans may destroy nature in the process of making themselves comfortable. In that case, nature will destroy us because nature is more powerful. If we do not make ourselves comfortable, nature can still make us extinct, like many species which did not evolve. If nature evolves humans further, it means humans have lost their freedom. Then humans are no more humans.

Spiritual Evolution

God has given humans a passive soul by design so that man tries to make the soul active. This is the ultimate awareness, also called self- realization. Self-realization is beyond the body and mind. It can be perceived but cannot be described. Hence, self-realization falls in the domain of mystics, not scientists. The journey towards self-realization is an individual effort. It can neither be enforced nor done collectively. It must begin within and at one's own initiative. Humans take pleasure in the pursuit of the affairs of the body and mind. All these affairs will perish when life comes to an end. What is permanent and cannot perish at all has not captured the fancy of most human beings.

Lamarck and Darwin had focused on physical evolution. Freud, Aurobindo and Maslow had stressed on mental evolution. The Eastern Philosophy has stressed on the evolution of the soul—a step-wise journey of the soul, starting from the lower creatures on the ladder and progressing first to plants, then to animals, humans and finally, to the supramental humans, where soul becomes active and drops the mind. As there is no mind, the soul does not enter a body. It gets liberated from the cycle of birth and death. This completes its evolution. Since man has been neglecting the pursuit of the soul, he is not evolving further. Awareness to pursue the soul is the secret for wellness in the future.

Evolution of Intuition

Intuition is to know without the use of the natural process of reasoning. It is a flash of understanding that comes after you have exhausted your efforts and reasoning. Intellect gives you scientific knowledge within the capability of the five senses. Intuition gives wisdom through the sixth sense. It is a revelation from the cosmic mind. Your might gives knowledge. Almighty gives wisdom. Spiritual wellness is the transit point from science to mysticism. Science is observation. Mysticism is beyond observation. Blissfulness and godliness happen when reasoning stops. In the state of blissfulness, you get flashes of wisdom, but not complete wisdom. In godliness, complete wisdom comes in a flash. Wisdom starts from blissfulness and ends in godliness. This is God-realization. After this is 'nirvana', meaning liberation, and 'moksha', meaning released from the cycle of birth and death. This is the end of human evolution.

Evolution has brought humans up to the level of knowledge. Further evolution from knowledge to wisdom is only possible through human efforts. Since many have achieved this wisdom, it is possible for others too. The wellness way of life offers the way ahead.

WELLNESS WAY OF LIFE

Why fall sick and then look for a cure?

The wellness way of life creates an environment to keep you healthy. Bruce Lipton in his book, *The Biology of Belief*, has brought out that the environment in which one lives has a strong influence on how genes function. He has scientifically demonstrated this aspect, which was intuitively known during Vedic times in India and practised as collective effort.

Collective Effort

Social Order

The society was broadly divided into four groups: the teacher, the warrior, the wealth maker and the worker. The wise taught, the warriors protected, the wealth makers traded goods produced by the workers. People were born and brought up in a controlled environment. The understanding was that this social environment would help them in refining their work, so that they would excel in their field of activity. This excellence would provide happiness, health and harmony. Their mind and body would remain at peace, because of which the soul would become more apparent.

This system, called '*varan*' (derived from '*vatavaran*' which means environment), was a horizontal division where nobody was superior or inferior. Gradually, it turned into a vertical caste-based division. Superior and inferior segregations crept in, which made the system oppressive, and thus, it lost its meaning.

At the individual level, life span was divided into four periods called ashramas. The first, *brahmacharya* (bachelorhood), was for learning, the second, *grihastha* (family life), was for earning, the third was *vaanprastha* (renunciation from active life) for returning and the fourth, *sanyaas* (dwelling in solitude), was for retreat. In the first 25 years, one learnt about '*kama*' (desires), '*arth*' (money), '*dharma*' (soul or true nature) and '*moksha*' (salvation). The next 25 years were dedicated to the pursuit of desires and money. In the third quarter, one pursued dharma and returned to the society by teaching, and sharing the knowledge and experiences, of indulging in desires and money. In the last quarter, one retreated from all attachments and worldly pursuits, to practice dharma exclusively to attain moksha. This division created a focus and environment to maintain wellness till the last day of life. In the first 50 years of life, people used their vigour and vitality to learn and earn. As age caught up, the activities which were less taxing and needed less energy were taken up. In the last ashrama, one would practise retreat from all kinds of attachment, so one could exit the present life for a peaceful next birth. However, with time these ashramas became too restrictive and rigid.

Religious Order

There have been many individuals like Buddha, Mahavira, Jesus, Zarathustra, Mohammed, who have tried to attain peace individually and shared their wisdom later with the world. They became the torch bearers and focal points for various religions. Religions again became a collective effort and have not produced the desired results.

Confucian Approach

Confucius suggested another way of collective effort. He proposed that the healer should be responsible for keeping the individual healthy. He said, 'A doctor should be paid to keep the person healthy. If the person becomes unhealthy, the doctor's fee should be deducted.' The idea that prevention is better than cure was the basis of wellness. The onus was not on the individual. Hence, this approach did not last for a long time.

The concept that prevention is better than cure, though thousands of years old, needs to be revived. But since there is no glamour and money making involved in prevention, it finds very minimal support. The glamour and money is in treating anything and everything once it manifests, not before that.

Individual Effort

In view of the above, individual effort in controlling one's environment is likely to be more successful. It suits the free will of the humans and shifts the onus of wellness on the individual. The wellness way of life does not interfere with any religion, ethics and morality laid down by the society. Hence, it can be implemented by everyone.

Air, water, food, thoughts, emotions, space and trillions of microorganisms that live in our body make our environment. Let us regulate them. There are some general points that must be emphasised here before we discuss specific activities for the body, mind, prana and soul.

Identify the Cause of Unwellness

Wellness eludes most people despite their wish to enjoy it. The cause is within you. Look within to see why you are not well. Irrespective of the cause, adopt a holistic approach to involve all aspects of wellness in your effort. Piecemeal efforts towards one aspect will not give you sustained wellness.

Love yourself

Loving yourself implies accepting and embracing all aspects of your being—the good, the bad and the ugly. Do not deny any part. Instead, improve upon what you are not accepting. Do not look for reasons to love you. You are breathing, which means the existence loves you, is a sufficient reason to love yourself. Unless you love yourself, you cannot love others and create an atmosphere of love that will heal you. If you do not love yourself, then you will not have a strong desire to attain a state of wellness. Strengthen your desire.

Stay Motivated to Fulfil the Desire

Staying young, attractive, energetic, calm, collected and creative is the reward of wellness. It makes living a pleasure.

Live in the Moment as Fully as Possible

Do not dwell in the past for it is gone. Do not live in the future for it is yet to come. Use your present to plan for future, but do not worry about its unfolding just the way you have planned. This will relieve you from the weight of the past and expectations of the future. Likewise, when performing an activity, stay engaged in it while it is happening and do not even think about it later. If you are doing anything absentmindedly, then you are not living in the moment. Be mindful even while performing routine activities, like eating, bathing, walking, talking, even breathing. Watch everything that you do, only then you are living in the moment.

Be Alert and Relaxed

Closely observe every activity that you are performing, and also watch that you are relaxed while performing it.

Enjoy What you are Doing

Enjoyment activates the pleasure centre in the brain and

releases dopamine. In an experiment involving the study of pain in rats, electrodes accidentally got placed close to the pleasure centre in the rat's brain. The rat was then put on a hot plate. It was observed that the rat did not feel any pain even when the temperature was raised to the point of burning. Electrodes had activated the pleasure centre to such an extent that the feeling of pain was not felt at all. There is only one example in human history where probably the pleasure centre was activated wilfully. Guru Arjan Dev, the fifth Sikh guru, was tortured by rulers of that time by making him sit on a hot iron plate. Guruji went through the ordeal stoically and did not feel any pain.

Break the Habits that Make you Unwell

Identify these habits, so you can change them. Maintain change for 21 days as it is believed that it takes that long to break a habit.

Synchronize with the Rhythm of Existence

Energies of the universe rise in the morning. This is evident from the blossoming of flowers, the chirping of birds, golden rays of Sun and the cool breeze. These energies ebb by the evening when plants and animals prepare to rest. Everybody does not have the same rhythm. Become aware of your rhythm, and if possible, synchronize it with nature.

Build a Routine

Routine gives regularity. It affects the body clock immensely by fixing the circadian rhythm that regulates all aspects of our physiology. The body gets attuned to the same activity at a particular time. When the body is prepared for an activity, it cooperates easily, enjoys more and is highly receptive. As a result, the benefits are tremendous. If you are new to the wellness way of life, follow your routine for at least three months. The impact on your wellness will give you the incentive to continue.

Practise Discipline

Discipline is absolutely necessary to follow the routine you set for yourself. It can override the tendency of shirking. It is possible that your routines may get compromised sometimes. Such situations should be accommodated without rigidity. If a part of the routine has been missed, rather than cramping it into the next item, it is better to drop it totally and continue with the next item.

Practise Patience

Patience and perseverance are virtues to attain wellness. Maintain a steady pace. Nothing can be achieved in a hurry, not even if you double up the efforts. Be consistent and continue the activities for wellness. Repetitions bring permanent changes in the body, mind and prana. A soft rope makes a groove in the stone by constantly rubbing the stone.

Avoid Complacency

Complacency is the enemy of wellness. Human frailties are such that once a person enjoys the comfort, he becomes complacent.

The wellness state is the time to religiously follow your lifestyle. Sant Kabir has said:

> 'Dukh mein sumiran sab karein, sukh mein kare na koye,
> Jo sukh mein sumiran kare to dukh kahe ko hoye.'

Everybody remembers God in times of distress and forgets him in the good times. If you continue to remember him at all times, then why there will be discomfort?

Customize your Lifestyle

No two individuals are identical in their physical and mental composition. Our reactions to exercise, food and weather, etc., are very distinct. Thus, we must customize activities to suit our specific needs.

Pursue the Golden Middle

The pursuit of wellness involves balancing several factors. As a result, one may experience physical, mental, emotional and spiritual stress. Physical and mental stress is easy to treat. Give rest to the body and mind. Emotional stress is difficult because it needs deep contemplation. Spiritual stress is the most difficult. It is almost madness to desire things which nobody has seen and there is no proof. People escape from the world to feel their soul and God. It is, thus, pertinent to aspire for the golden middle. If you go beyond your limits in the pursuit of wellness, then you are violent to your body. Violence vitiates vitality. Violence invites virulence which causes disease.

Develop a Knack for Listening to the Body and Mind

This is the most significant aspect of developing a wellness way of life. Develop watchfulness to do it. Recognize the first innocuous looking signs and symptoms of discomfort or disease. Do not suppress this expression, attend to it.

Why the Wellness Way of Life?

According to Greek mythology, the divine has endowed all living beings with Eros and Thanatos. Eros means creation or the 'Vishnu aspect' as per Hindu mythology and Thanatos means destruction or the 'Shiva aspect'. Eros comes from the soul because the soul is permanent and gives us the spark to lead a long life that can go on and on, quite like the soul. Thanatos comes from the body because the body knows that it can never be permanent. It must wither and perish no matter what we do. Eros gives us the desire to maintain our body. Thanatos encourages overindulgence and passivity in us. Whether we increase Eros or Thanatos is our choice. The wellness way of life aims to increase Eros and decrease Thanatos.

Life is sustained by a delicate balance which may get disturbed by anything that does not go well with your body and mind. It can be an emotion, a thought, lack of exercise, wrong food or unhealthy eating habits, weather, your environment—including companions, family and friends, society, plants, animals and even distant stars and planets, etc. The imbalance does not become serious in a day. It takes time to build up before you land up with the doctor. The wellness way of life prepares you to identify this imbalance, so that it can be intercepted much before it causes disease. If despite your sincere efforts the imbalance lingers on, then consult your doctor immediately because a stitch in time saves nine.

Humans do not live in natural environments anymore. From living in open spaces outside, we have now moved inside. No wonder wellness does not come to us naturally. We need to have a structured way of life that enhances wellness. While most humans choose pleasure over wellness, the wellness lifestyle curbs this tendency.

PART II

PRACTISING WELLNESS

WATCHFULNESS

Be a spectator to the drama of your life

Watchfulness implies paying attention to yourself, to what you are doing at the physical, mental, pranic, and spiritual level. Normally you do not watch what you are doing. You remain unaware. By practising watchfulness, you are doing something and seeing it too. You become aware. Awareness, witnessing, mindfulness, observation and watch- fulness are synonymous. Watching outside is instinctive. It works as an armour to enable survival. Watching within is intellective. It is elective. It is a choice, so it is nascent and needs to be cultivated. Only humans can watch their own body and mind. It is a special privilege of man, but it is rarely used.

What is within you that watches? It is the soul. The soul watching your body-mind is watchfulness. In doing so, your soul becomes a 'seer' and both your body and mind become 'seen'. When this separation between the 'seer' and the 'seen' becomes evident only then you can understand yourself and your life from a new perspective. If it has not happened in your life, then you have missed something of tremendous value.

How to Develop Watchfulness?

Sit silently in a relaxed state, doing nothing, and watchfulness will happen. However, it is easier said than done.

Another way is to watch what you are doing, and you will become watchful. Watch all your actions minutely. While bathing, observe your hand movements, feel the flow of water, observe the rubbing of the body. While eating, observe every small action. While walking, observe your left foot rising and the right foot on the ground. Feel the breeze on your face. Similarly, while running, observe the way you run. Small actions from your daily life can be turned into watchful practices and gradually, you will stay watchful even while doing more serious work. The periods of unawareness when you are not watchful will still creep in. Welcome these as a contrast to the periods when you were watchful.

Dhyana

The best way you can develop watchfulness is by learning *'dhyana'*. It is a Sanskrit word, which further refines watchfulness. It is pronounced as *'chyan'* by Zen practitioners. *Chyan* gradually became *'chin'*. It is natural for all of us to watch what is happening outside us. However, we do not care to look within. This is where dhyana comes into play. Dhyana means paying attention to yourself. Attention can be active and passive. Active attention means acting and reacting to what you are watching. Passive attention means only being a witness; you neither act nor react. Passive watching is dhyana. It is neutral. While watching, you remain free from all value judgements. In fact, this neutrality continues even after the process of watching. You do not get attached to the object being watched. This detached observation creates a distance between you and what you are watching. Normally your mind does not allow you to do neutral watching. However, the practice of dhyana gradually overcomes the mind, and you reach a state of 'No mind'. Then you become aware of your soul. This awareness turns the passive observer, your soul, into an active one. Active soul becomes a link between the body-mind and itself. Now your soul can witness your physical and mental activity. Once this is done, it is easy to withdraw from outside and turn inwards. The more you look within, the more you start to understand yourself. Here is how you can practise dhyana:

Technique

Sit in chin mudra

Place your hands on the knees in such a way that your wrist joints should rest on them, with the palms facing upwards. Keep your arms straight but relaxed. Touch the index finger and thumb gently at the tip.

Keep the other fingers open and relaxed. Keep the facial muscles relaxed. Keep the spine erect but not tensed. Push the lower part of the spine forward to keep the spine erect. Be alert and do not let the spine sag at any time during the whole

Figure 6. Sitting in chin mudra

process. Adjust the body to the most comfortable position because after this you should be motionless.

Make the body still

Practise stillness by involving the mind. When the mind instructs, the body obeys. Your willpower shall keep your body still. For the first few days, observe your body sitting still and observe for how long it can do so. If it moves, again make it still. Overpower the desire, compulsion and reason that causes the body to move. This way you will improve your willpower.

Consciously breathe in and breathe out

Breathe in slowly to the mental count of five. Then hold your breath. Observe the pause for a second. Now exhale till the count of five. Pause for a second and observe the pause. Follow the breath going in and going out. Feel the coolness of air in the nostrils while inhaling. Feel the warmth of air in the nostrils while exhaling. Repeat this process five times. You can keep a count on the left hand. Now let the body resume its normal breathing.

Observe the body

This is done in three stages:

Become aware of the touch of the index finger with the thumb. Make the touch so light and gentle that it is barely felt. Observe it for one minute or so.

Observe the natural rhythm of your breathing. Be aware of your breath going in and out at its own pace. Become conscious of your natural breathing. Do not make any effort to breathe consciously as you had done earlier. This observation needs more attention than touch. But it enhances your power of watching even more.

Listen to your heartbeat. It needs even more attention. It is the most subtle part of the natural body function.

This gradual process of observing the body will progressively sharpen your power of watching. Practice this observation for three- four minutes. The body is being seen by the observer. Let it sink in you that there is a distance between the observer and the body. Feel that distance. This feeling will make your faculty of observation strong and convince you that the observer is distinct from your body.

Observe your thoughts

When the body becomes still, the mind becomes more apparent. It becomes easy to observe thoughts. Thoughts are even more subtle than the heartbeat. While the heartbeat can be felt, our thoughts are a phenomenon of the mind and are not as apparent. Here is how one can observe one's thoughts:

How often does a thought cross your mind? Observe the rapid flow of thoughts one after the other. They are like speeding vehicles on the road. Just as there is a gap between two vehicles, there is also a gap between two thoughts. Look for this gap. Though it may not be noticed initially, stay at it. The goal is to observe these thoughts and gradually prolong the gap between two thoughts. As the gap grows, the frequency of thoughts slows down. These gaps represent moments of tranquillity and inner calm because the mind is at rest. It is important to become aware that in watching the thoughts and gaps, the observer in you is separate from both. Let this feeling sink in again. This will make your soul stronger and more apparent to you.

What comprises your thoughts? Analyse the quality of your thoughts—both positive and negative. Do not pass any judgement, be neutral. Do not identify with them; remember you are only a witness. Do not get involved with the quality of thoughts. Let them come and go. Remain an observer to their flow. Stay detached and aloof from the quality of thoughts. Enjoy the feeling of aloofness. This will train the observer to be more powerful. Practise this observation for three–four minutes.

Observe your emotions

This is the most subtle part of watchfulness. While thoughts are material and can be watched, emotions are feelings and can only be felt.

They are real even if they are not material. Emotions are deep seated, so you will have to go deep within to look for obvious and hidden emotions. You will have to withdraw your observation from all else and keenly search for your emotions.

There are both negative and positive emotions. Any emotion that dampens your spirits is negative, such as sadness, hatred, anguish, jealousy, hurt, vengeance. Witness the emotion surfacing in your mind. Allow it to come into your observation. Do not hold it; instead, wilfully release it into the space. See it bursting like a bubble. Feel a heavy weight being lifted off yourself. Cherish the lightness.

Similarly, look for positive emotions. Any emotion that perks up your mood is positive, such as happiness, joy, ecstasy. However, these are also burdens. They are weighty and influence us. Release them in the space. Feel the neutrality of an emotionless state. Stay in this space for some time (three–four minutes) before moving to the next stage.

Observe the observer

When the mind is still the soul becomes apparent. The soul has been observing the body, thoughts and emotions. Now let the soul observe itself. This is a state where there is no content to observe. There is no choice with you to select what to observe. There is only pure consciousness. There is the observer but nothing to observe. This is your soul observing itself.

Watchfulness cannot go beyond the state of observation. Beyond it is meditation. It happens of its own accord. It is a reward for those who have completed the previous steps. You are awakened. It is a very delicate phase of dhyana. Some days it comes naturally and easily while on other days it does not come at all. Gradually, the days it comes naturally will increase. In this state there is no awareness of the body, thoughts and emotions. This is the state of bliss. Let this state stay for as long as it lasts. Feel blissful, connected with the entire universe, and feel the harmony. Beyond this is God, the unknowable.

Why Watchfulness?

Watchfulness awakens your soul. You can notice the minutest change in your body. You can register every ripple in your mind. You can reach the dark recesses and higher levels of the mind. Unwellness cannot creep in surreptitiously. You will know what you are doing. Knowingly, you cannot do any wrong.

Watchfulness makes you see that the observer is the same, but the objects of observation—the body and mind—change. They are temporary, hence insignificant.

Watchfulness makes you responsive and not reactive. Response is a thoughtful action. Reaction is a knee jerk action. When you are watchful, you do not suppress but express in a way that does not offend the other.

Watchfulness is the key to successful implementation of wellness way of life. Make watchfulness a constant, a second nature, a habit even in adversity.

Practising Watchfulness when Unwell

Use unwellness as an opportunity to practise watchfulness. Look at your body. There is pain, discomfort and suffering, but you can look at it. Observe that there is a distance between you and the body. Observe your mind and emotions during sickness. Watch how they have disturbed your wellness. See how unwellness has started. The cause will come up. Being watchful during unwellness will reveal to you that sickness has happened to your body and mind, but not to your soul.

WAY TO PHYSICAL WELLNESS

Physique is facade

The physical body is the most convenient layer to start one's journey of practising the wellness way of life. Physical wellness is regulated by one's genes. Genes go on working, whether you are sick or healthy, to produce proteins that make and mend your body. You cannot change your genes, but you can influence their environment to quite an extent, so that the genes can function to their optimum potential. Modify your physical posture, exercises, bathing, eating, drinking, biome, pooping, sleeping and talking. In addition, energize the body with massages and body packs. They maintain dynamism of the body and have a profound effect on its wellness. Stay watchful during all your physical activities. It will keep your mind in the moment and give respite from its wanderings.

Wellness Posture and Manners

Posture of the body and your mannerisms give the first impression about your physical wellness. Maintain a youthful posture and pleasing manners. They add up to your appearance.

Pay attention to your posture. Straighten your back, hold

your head high, pull in the chin, throw the chest out and keep the shoulders broad. This will drastically change your appearance. Do not shuffle your feet while walking. Walk with a stride that exudes confidence. Walk smartly and briskly like a young person. Watch your posture all the time while sitting, standing, walking, eating, talking and relaxing.

How to Improve Posture?

Stand or sit next to a wall. Touch your shoulders with the wall. Now touch the back of your head with the wall. There may be stiffness initially, but gradually your body will adjust. Repeat this exercise till you can hold the posture naturally while walking, sitting or standing.

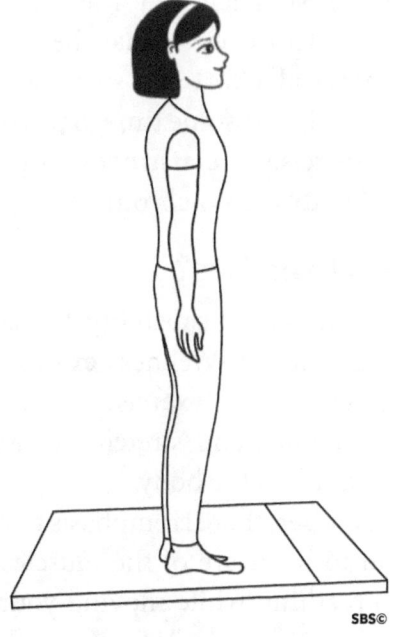

Figure 7. Body posture

WELLNESS EXERCISES

Movement makes you dynamic

Animals indulge in sufficient physical activity in the pursuit of food and mate. However, human beings no longer need to undertake physical effort for such pursuits. Thus, it is imperative for us to invest some time in physically moving our body. Wellness exercises are a structured physical activity in which mind and body are synchronized.

Why Wellness Exercises?

The body has remarkable capability to resist the onset of disease and reverse it too. Wellness exercises augment these therapeutic powers. These exercises move all joints, twist and turn the backbone, and stretch all muscles. This lends suppleness and agility to the body.

During the exercises, there is emphasis to watch movements of the body and to be aware of the muscles being stretched. Observe your breathing while moving your body as well as on assuming the final position of exercise. This watchfulness withdraws your attention from worries and problems, at least for the period of exercise and helps relax the mind.

An optimistic and enjoyable attitude during wellness

exercises activates the pleasure centre in the brain. This releases dopamine and endorphin, which create a sense of well-being that lasts for 24 hours. That is why one should exercise daily.

Complete participation of the body and mind in wellness exercises changes the mental and emotional makeup, which brings peace and tranquillity. The exercises relax a person physically as well as mentally.

Wellness exercises help conserve and enhance your energy without tiring you out, so you can practise these till the last days of your life. This is its advantage over sports. In games, focus is on the others. In wellness exercises, it is on yourself. You compete only with yourself to improve your postures. This gives a taste of self-actualization.

Minor Exercises

These exercises are meant for the sick, convalescing, elderly and as a starter for those who have never exercised earlier. These can be comfortably done even in bed.

Exercise arms while sitting

  i. Stretch the arms forward.
  ii. Clench the hands into fists. Clench hard and release pressure.
  iii. Open the palms and spread out the fingers as wide as possible.
  iv. Turn the wrist joints clockwise and then anticlockwise.
  v. Bend the arms at the elbow joints, press your lower arms on the upper arms and return.
  vi. Raise both arms on the sides at shoulder level and bring them down.
  vii. Raise both arms above your head. Make them straight to touch the ears and bring them down.
  viii. Turn the upper body to the left. Hold for some time, then move to the right and hold for some more time.

Exercise legs while sitting

  i. Stretch the legs in front.

ii. Clench the feet and relax.
iii. Move the ankle joints up and down. Rotate them clockwise and anticlockwise. Come to normal position.
iv. Bend your left leg at the knee and press the lower leg with the upper leg. Make the leg straight. Do the same with the right leg.
v. Bend both legs at the knees and press the lower legs with the upper legs. Make the legs straight.

While lying

i. Fold the right leg and gently press the abdomen. Hold for some time and return.
ii. Fold the left leg and gently press the abdomen. Hold for some time and return.
iii. Fold both the legs together and gently press the abdomen. Hold for some time and return.
iv. Raise one leg up and bring it down. Repeat with the other leg.
v. Raise both legs together and bring them down.

Initially, practise each exercise five times, and gradually increase it to ten times. Breathe deeply and slowly all along. Watch all the movements. In one week, you will regain your strength and be able to do these exercises while standing and subsequently take up moderate exercises.

Moderate Exercises

Wellness walk

Walking is to humans as flying is to birds and swimming is to fish. It is natural and suitable even for those who are not used to physical activity.

Walk in silence

Lao Tzu used to go for morning walk alone. Quite often, his close friend would request him to be taken along, but Lao

Tzu would decline. Since the friend continued to insist, Lao Tzu relented with the condition that there would not be any talking while walking. Both started going together for a 'walk in silence'. One day, as the Sun rose, the friend could not hold his ecstasy and said, 'What a beautiful sunrise!' Lao Tzu did not respond at that time, but on returning, he told the gentleman not to accompany him henceforth. Just one sentence in a few months was enough to interrupt Lao Tzu's meditative walk.

Watch your walk

Watch your feet while walking. Observe the left foot rising from the ground while the right foot is on the ground, and then see the right foot moving and the left one touching the ground. Watch the heel touching the ground first, then the sole and the toes.

Observe nature all around

Enjoy the colours, hues, noises and sounds of nature. Large open spaces, vegetation, chirping of birds and the rays of Sun will shake off your lethargy. Feel the breeze and sunshine on your face. This is the divine touching you. Paying attention to nature will help take your mind off the thoughts and emotions. It will keep you in the present moment and make walking meditative.

Walk for 20 minutes or more at a steady pace. You can also practise slow walk for the first five minutes and brisk walk for the next five minutes. Continue alternating with both for the allotted time. Walking can be done at any time of the day or night.

Wellness run

Run at a slow speed for a short distance as per your strength. Stop if you feel any discomfort. Then walk briskly or slowly for the same distance. This way you will not harm yourself while running. Practise only two laps for the first few days, and then gradually increase as per your capacity. Bring your attention to your legs while running, just as in walking (discussed above) to make it meditative.

Major Exercises

These exercises are for those who are reasonably fit. We have practised these for many years and found them to be very effective. Consult your doctor before starting these exercises. Do not practise when you are ill, even in mild cold or diarrhoea.

Prerequisites

The best time to exercise is before breakfast. Else, wait for three hours after taking food. Go to the toilet and ease yourself if possible. Wear loose, light clothes for free movement.

Use an anti-slip mat, a blanket or rug. Do not use a sponge mattress or bare floor. Choose an airy, clean, quiet and dry place without any foul smell.

Regularity and consistency is the key to good results

Exercise in the same place, at the same time and for the same period that suits you. Doing one long session and then taking a break for a few days does not give any benefits.

Do not tire yourself

Start with simple exercises, and gradually move to the difficult ones. Do not use excessive force to reach the final position. It will come by practice as the body becomes flexible. The least force you use, the better is the result.

Stay within your comfort zone

If you feel slight sweat on your forehead, it is an indication that you have reached your limit of tolerance. At the end of the session, you should feel more energetic, calm and strong, both physically and mentally. If you are feeling tired or experience any discomfort, then something may be wrong with your exercise. Consult an expert to demonstrate the exercises mentioned in this chapter to understand where you are lacking.

Be relaxed

The emphasis is on stretching the muscles in a relaxed manner. Tense muscles resist stretching. Relaxed muscles stretch automatically. Never hurry. If you are short of time, do a few practices only, but maintain a slow and relaxed pace. All movements from start to end should be slow, smooth and coordinated with breath to conserve energy and induce mental tranquillity. The immobility of the final posture and relaxed respiration produces profound and beneficial changes in the body.

Always breathe through nose and never through mouth

Take deep, slow and rhythmic breaths as far as possible. Be more aware of your breathing.

Feel the effect on the body

Try to be aware of the posture, your mental makeup, attitude, thoughts and emotions. Count four breaths in the final position. Then return to the original position. Feel the body settling after it has returned to the original position. Repeat the exercise only after the body is settled.

Do not dilute, divert or interrupt your exercise period by indulging in any other activity, howsoever small or insignificant. Postpone all other activities. Once you have taken position on the mat, bring the body and the mind in the mood to exercise. Mentally repeat the following to yourself:

> I will watch all movements of my body.
> I will bring my awareness to the parts of my body that get stretched.
> I will watch my breathing during movement, on attaining the final position, and during the rest position as well.
> I will watch the body settling after every exercise.

Standing exercises
Vertical stretch

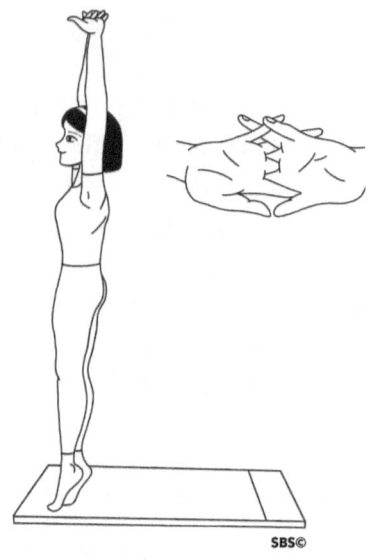

Figure 8. Vertical stretch

Stand with the feet together or six inches apart. Keep your eyes fixed on a point in front. It will help in maintaining balance. Interlock your fingers. Breathe in and slowly raise your interlocked hands above your head. Invert the hands so that the palms are facing the sky or the ceiling. Watch your breathing and your movement. Touch the muscles of your upper arms with ears. Stretch the whole body vertically. Simultaneously raise your feet and rest on your toes. Feel the stretch in your arms, shoulder, chest, abdomen, spine, legs and feet. Stay in this position till the count of four–five breaths. Become aware of the final stretch and breathing. Once you feel that you have fully stretched, try to stretch a little more, but do not lose balance. This further stretching will make you intensely watchful. Now slowly bring your hands down while exhaling and bring your heels on the ground. Watch this movement. Watch the exhalation. It takes a count of two–three breaths to settle down. Repeat once it has settled.

Sideways stretch

Figure 9. Sideways stretch

Keep the feet three feet apart. Keep them straight and parallel to the edge of the mat as shown in Figure 10. Normally, when we stand, the feet are at an angle. Inhale and raise the arms sideways in line with your shoulders and parallel to the ground. Keep the palms open. While breathing in, raise the right arm up. Touch the muscle of the upper arm to the right ear. Now stretch the arm further upwards. Breathe out and bend the body to the left side and bring the left arm down on the left leg. Do not rest left arm on the left leg. Keep the right arm straight over the head. Do not let it bend at the elbow. Maintain this position for four counts of normal breathing. Feel the stretch on the right side of the trunk. Breathe in and raise the body up. Simultaneously bring the arms in line with the shoulders. Now breathe out and bring the arms down. Observe the movement of the arms throughout. Feel the body settling down and then repeat on the left side. Do it twice.

Spine twist

Figure 10. Spine twist

Maintain the position of feet as stated above. Keep your arms, shoulders and spine relaxed. Raise the arms sideways in line with shoulders and parallel to the ground. Inhale and bring the arms in front at shoulder height and parallel to the ground, making sure that your palms are open. Keep the palms facing each other and shoulder distance apart. Maintain this distance between the palms while turning the trunk and arms to the right and left. Exhale and turn the trunk to the right. Also turn the neck, head and eyes to the right and look behind as much as possible. Breathe normally and maintain this position for four–five breaths. Now inhale and come to the front. Exhale and turn to the left side. Be aware of the movement, your breathing and the stretch in the whole spine. Do it twice on each side. Then bring the arms to the sides and bring them down. Feel the body settling down before doing the next exercise.

One-leg balance

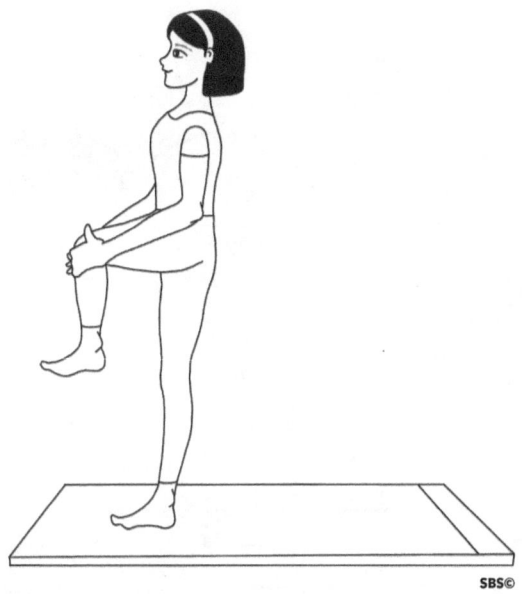

Figure 11. One-leg balance

Stand erect. Keep your feet one foot apart. Stand on the right leg. Breathe in and fold the left leg at the knee while bringing it up so that the thigh is parallel to the ground and the lower part of the leg is perpendicular to the floor. Hold the left knee in interlocked hands. Do not bring the shoulders forward. Keep the eyes fixed on a point in front. Focus on that point as that will help you in maintaining balance. Maintain the position to the count of three–four breaths. Breathe out while bringing the leg down. Feel the body settling. Repeat balancing on the left leg. Do it twice. Maintain normal breathing while balancing. You may experience some initial difficulty, but you will improve gradually if you stay at it. Any thoughts that compete for your attention and take your mind away from this exercise will make you lose balance.

Abdomen press

These are of three types:

Type I

Figure 12. Abdomen press type I

Keep your feet one foot apart. Slightly bend at the knees and hold your thighs just above the knees. Keep your arms straight. Exhale fully and hold the breath. Pull your abdomen towards the spine as much as you can. Hold it and count till 10 or more as per your comfort. Look in front while holding the position. Stop holding the breath and release the contraction in the abdomen. Breathe in deeply, straighten the knees and stand erect. Feel the body settling down. It takes more time than other exercises to settle. Breathe normally till you feel comfortable. Repeat once.

Type II

Make the same position as type I. Breathe out completely and hold the breath. Pull the stomach in, towards the spine and move it forward and backward vigorously 20 times. Keep looking in front. Stop holding the breath. Breathe in deeply and stand erect. Breathe normally. Repeat when comfortable.

Type III

Take the same position as above. Look in front. Exhale and hold your breath. Move the abdomen towards the spine. Now push the central portion of the abdomen forward. Hold it there and move the central portion in a circle from right to left. Initially, you may move your body slightly to help the abdomen move. Do it five times. Then repeat the same from left to right five more times. Stop holding the breath and relax the abdomen. Breathe in deeply and stand erect. Maintain normal breathing till comfortable. Repeat once.

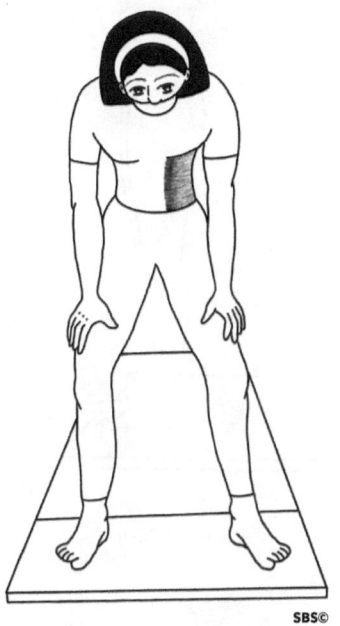

Figure 13. Abdomen press type III

Whole body stretch

This exercise involves continuous stretching of the whole body, but it must be done step by step. Hold every step for one or two breaths. Move to the front edge of the mat for these stretches.

Step I

Stand erect with your feet together. Keep palms folded in front of the chest. Breathe normally. Relax the body and observe your breathing.

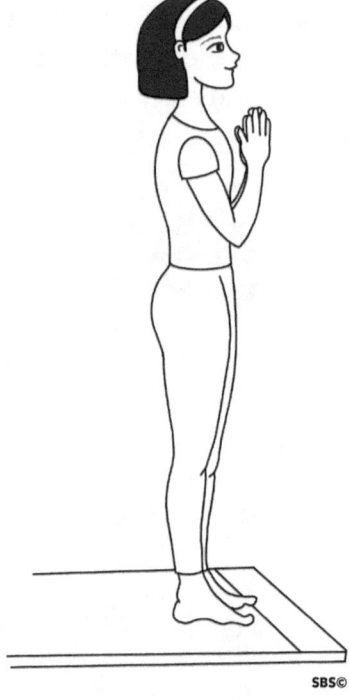

Figure 14. Step I

Step II

While breathing in, raise your arms above the head with open palms facing in front. Stretch the arms upwards and slightly bend the upper trunk backwards. Look up.

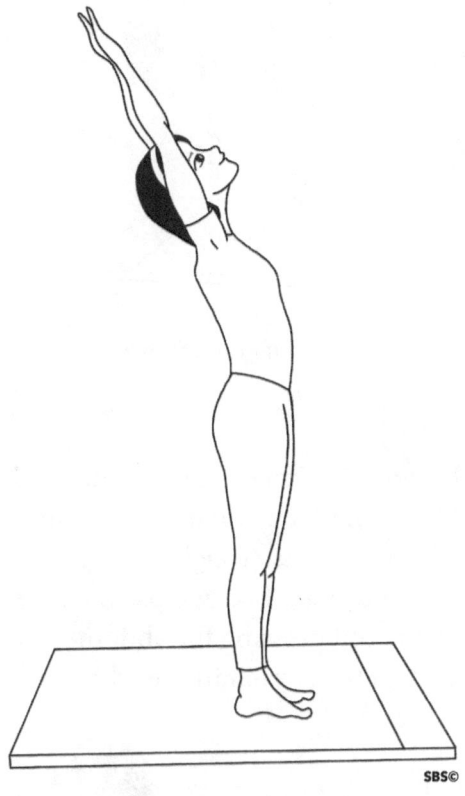

Figure 15. Step II

Step III

Exhale and bend forward gently, smoothly and slowly. Touch your hands to the ground or as near to it as possible. Do not overdo it. Keep the legs straight at knees. You may experience some initial difficulty, but you will improve gradually if you stay at it. Look towards your knees. Feel the stretch in the back side of the legs.

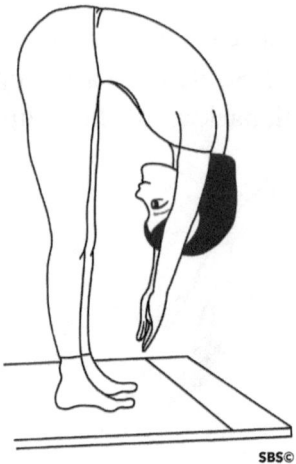

Figure 16. Step III

Step IV

Exhale and bend the knees slightly, keeping the palms on the outer side of the feet. Inhale deeply and move the right leg backwards. Keep it as straight as possible. Now push the pelvis forward and head backwards. Look upwards. The left knee will be bent and pressing the abdomen. Maintain normal breathing and feel the stretch in the whole body.

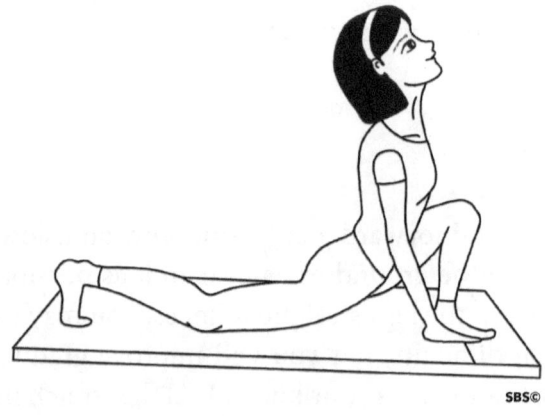

Figure 17. Step IV

Step V

Breathe in and move the left leg backwards to bring the feet together. Keep the spine straight. Support your body on toes and hands. Keep your arms straight and look in front. Feel the pressure on your arms and legs. Breathe normally.

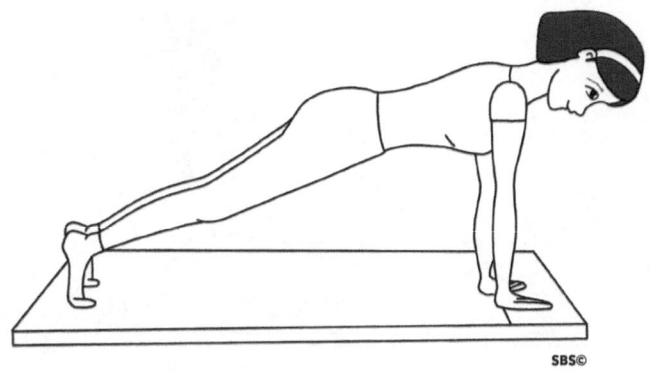

Figure 18. Step V

Step VI

Exhale and lower the body by bending the arms at elbows. Touch the knees first to the floor and then lower the chest to touch the ground. Touch the chin to the ground. Look in front. The pelvis and navel should not touch the ground. If they do, then lift the hips slightly above the ground. Breathe normally.

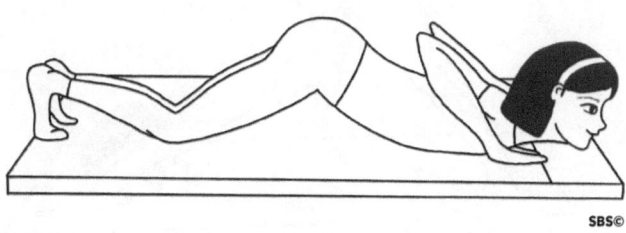

Figure 19. Step VI

Step VII

Exhale and lower the pelvis to the ground. Inhale and raise the trunk, but keep the navel touching the ground. Keep the arms slightly bent at elbows. Keep the elbows touching the body. Feel the weight on the arms. Be aware of the lower back. Breathe normally.

Figure 20. Step VII

Step VIII

Inhale and make the arms straight and raise the hips up. Move the head down between the arms. Look at the navel. Move the feet a step or two forward to try and keep the soles of the feet on ground as much as possible. Feel the stretch in the legs, arms and neck. Breathe normally.

Figure 21. Step VIII

Step IX

Inhale and move the right leg forward and place the right foot between the palms. Make the left leg straight as far as possible. Push the pelvis forward and head backwards. Look up. Breathe normally and feel the stretch in the whole body. It is the opposite of Step IV.

Step X

Exhale and move the left leg forward to bring the left foot near the right foot. Make the legs straight without bending on the knees. Keep the arms straight with fingers of open palms as near the floor as possible. Look towards the knees. Feel stretch in the backside of legs. Breathe normally. It is the same position as Step III.

Step XI

Inhale and raise the arms above the head and bend the back slightly. Look up. It is the same position as Step II.

Step XII

Return to Step I. Breathe normally. Bring the arms to the sides. Repeat the 12 steps only after the body has settled. For the first three days you may do these 12 steps only once. Then increase it to two for next three days, then to three in the next three days and maximum to four if you are doing other exercises too.

Sitting exercises

Rest position

Sit on the floor with your legs relaxed and arms at the back with palms on the floor. Breathe in slowly and deeply by expanding the abdominal muscles. Then fill the lungs further by expanding the chest muscles. Hold the breath for a second, then exhale slowly and completely, first by contracting the chest muscles and then abdominal muscles. Continue breathing like this for five–seven breaths.

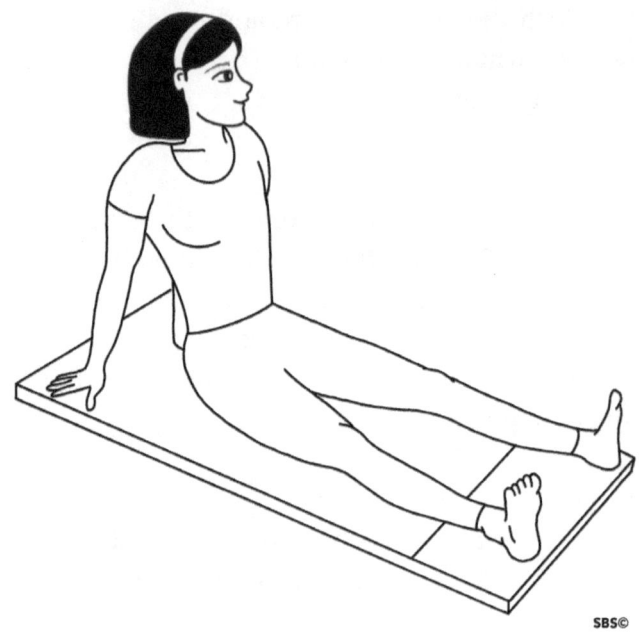

Figure 22. Rest position

Sit on heels

Kneel on the mat while keeping your knees together. Place the feet in such a way that the big toes touch each other. Keep your arms on the side of the body with palms on the floor. Now slowly lower your body to rest the hips on the heels. Sit on the heels. Initially it may be difficult. So, push the body upwards to transfer the weight on the hands. Gradually you will be able to do it. Keep the spine erect to keep the neck, head and torso in one line. Keep the shoulders broad and relaxed. Place your hands on the thighs. Feel the stretch on the thigh muscles and pressure on the lower legs. Close your eyes. Breathe normally and become aware of your breathing. Stay in this position for at least two minutes or less if there is discomfort. With practice it will become easier.

Figure 23. Sit on heels

Abdomen press

While sitting on your heels bring the arms in front. Clench your fists with thumbs raised. Place both the fists on the navel so that the knuckles and thumb are touching each other. Press the forearms on the abdomen. Now exhale as much as you can, and bring the trunk down on the thighs while pressing the abdomen with fisted hands. Look in front. Press more, and feel the pulsation of blood. Breathe normally and count till 10 or more. Inhale and raise the trunk to the starting position. Breathe normally till your body settles. Repeat once more.

Figure 24. Abdomen press

Forward bending of spine

Sit on the floor. Keep the legs stretched in front with feet joined together. Keep the spine erect. Inhale and raise the hands above your head. Bend slightly backwards and stretch the hands up. Exhale and lower hands to touch the toes with fingers. Look at the knees. Breathe normally. During every exhalation, try to bring the elbows near the knees. Feel the stretch in the whole body. After four breaths inhale and raise your hands above the head. Exhale and bring the hands down. Repeat once when the body settles.

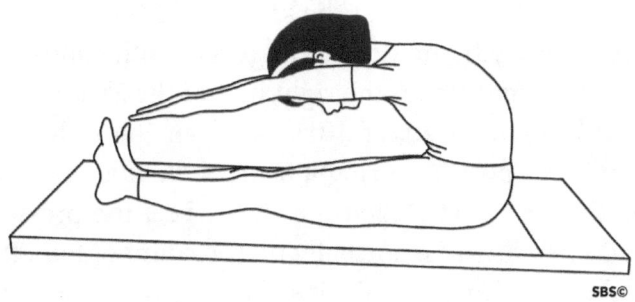

Figure 25. Forward bending of spine.

Exercises while lying on back

Horizontal stretching

Join your feet together. Bring arms to the sides of the body. Inhale and raise your hands and interlock the fingers. Raise the interlocked hands above the head and invert the hands. Now stretch the body as much as possible. Stretch a bit more once you feel that you have stretched fully. You will be surprised that it can stretch a bit more. Like that, stretch to the maximum. Breathe normally and feel the stretch in the whole body from hands to toes. Exhale after four or five breaths and bring the hands on the sides. Come to the normal position. Feel the body settling down. Repeat once more when the body has settled.

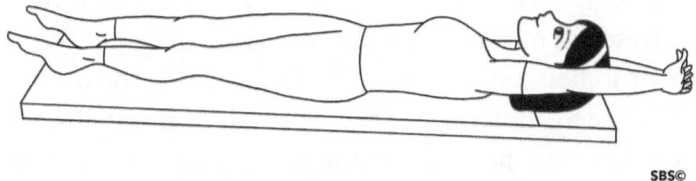

Figure 26. Horizontal stretching

Half abdomen press

Keep the left leg pressed on the floor. Inhale and raise the right leg straight up. Bend at the knee. Hold the right leg, just below the knee, with interlocked fingers of both hands. Exhale and press the right leg on the right half of the abdomen. Now inhale and lift the head, and try to touch the right knee to the chin. If not possible, bring it as near the knee as possible. Keep both the feet stretched outwards. Feel the pressure on your abdomen. Breathe normally till the count of four. Inhale, release the right leg and make it straight upwards. Exhale and bring the head down and then bring the leg down very slowly as that will stretch the abdomen. Feel the body settling. Repeat on the left side.

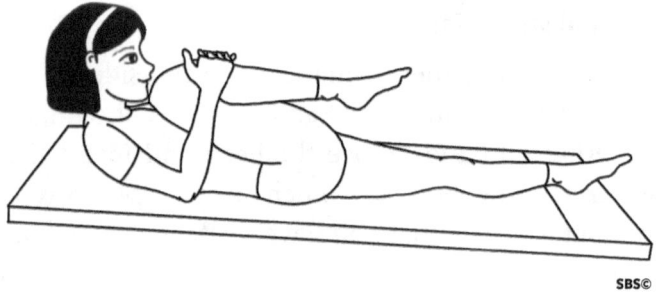

Figure 27. Half abdomen press

Full abdomen press

Inhale and lift both the legs simultaneously. Bend at the knees and hold the legs with both hands just below the knees. Exhale and press the legs to the abdomen. Keep the feet stretched outwards. Inhale and raise the head to bring it close or in between the knees if possible. Feel the pressure on the abdomen. Breathe normally till four counts. Inhale and release the legs and raise them straight upward. Exhale and bring the head down, and then slowly lower the legs. Feel the body settling. Repeat once.

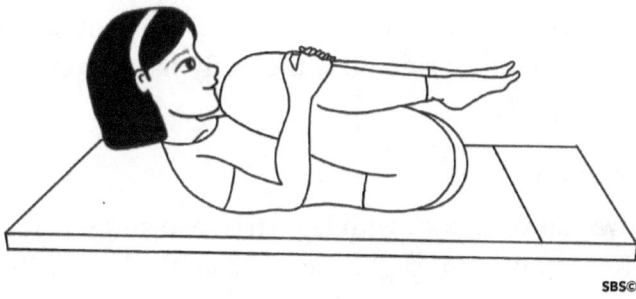

Figure 28. Full abdomen press

Sideways twist of spine

Spread your arms on the sides in line with your shoulders. Let the palms face upwards. Fold the right leg, and place the right foot near the left knee. Initially, you may keep the foot on the knee to make it easy. Inhale and place the left palm on the outer surface of the right knee. Exhale and guide the right knee to cross over the left leg, and gradually make the right knee touch the floor across the left leg. Simultaneously turn your head to right side and look at the right palm. Keep the right shoulder touching the ground. This is important to ensure twist to the whole spine. Hold the position with normal

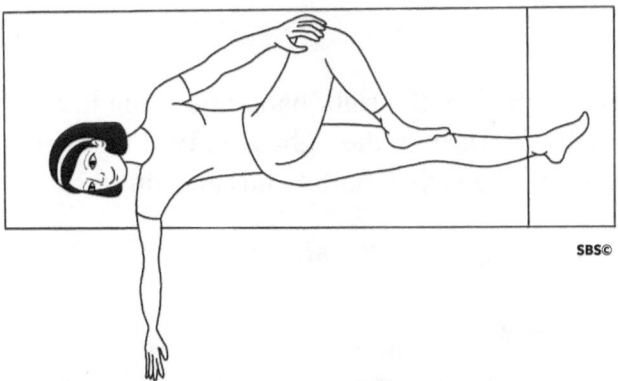

Figure 29. Sideways twist of spine

breathing. Count till four breaths and then return to the starting position. Breathe normally. Feel the body settling and repeat on the other side once the body has become normal. Do it twice.

Rest position

Lie down on your back with legs stretched and separated by a foot. Keep your arms slightly away from the body with palms open and facing upwards. Let the body weight sink to the floor. Become like a dead body. Feel that you are dead, and your soul is outside your body and looking at you. This is how it will be at the time of death. Feel the relaxation of the dead body rather than becoming scared of the feeling of death. Stay in this state of rest for a minute. The dead cannot think, so be silent in the mind too.

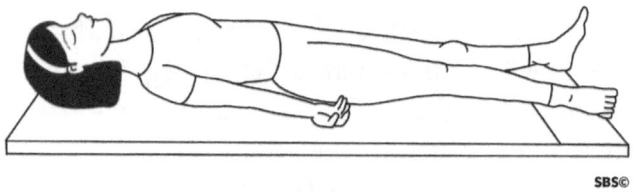

Figure 30. Rest position

To rise, first raise the right hand above the head. Fold the left leg halfway. Turn on the right side. Wait for a few seconds then rise with the help of both hands and sit.

Exercises while lying on the abdomen

Upper back bending

Lie down on the abdomen. Keep your feet together. Keep your arms on the side of the body. Interlock the hands and keep them on the back. Inhale and first raise the head and abdomen from the mat. Then raise the interlocked hands as much above the body as possible. Look up. Breathe normally till four breaths. Exhale and bring the head and abdomen on the mat and interlocked hands on the back. Breathe normally and repeat once the body has become normal. Do it twice.

Figure 31. Upper back bending

Lower back bending

Keep arms under the legs with palms facing thighs. Inhale deeply and raise both the legs up by one foot from the floor. Keep the feet together and stretch legs and feet outwards. Look in front. Breathe normally and hold this position up to the count of five breaths. Exhale and bring the legs down. Feel the effect on the heart and back of the body. Repeat when the body is settled.

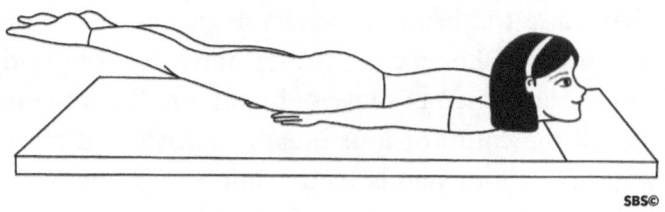

Figure 32. Lower back bending

Sideways twisting of back

Fold your arms, and place your palms on the sides of the shoulders. Keep the elbows in touch with the body. Spread the legs, and place the feet near the edge of the mat. Inhale and raise the upper part of the body up to the navel. Keep the navel in touch with the floor. Shift the weight of the body on the arms. Turn the head to the right side to look at the left heel. Breathe normally till the count of four. Exhale and lower the body. Breathe normally. Repeat on the left side once the body settles.

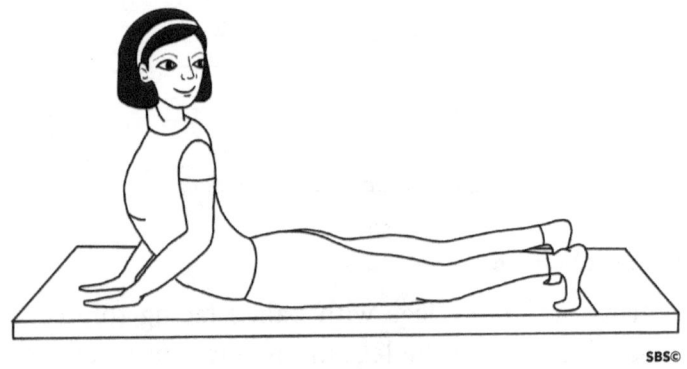

Figure 33. Sideways twisting of back.

Full bending of spine

Bring arms forward with palms open. Now fold the legs at the knees. Take the right hand backwards and hold the right ankle. Do same for left ankle. Inhale and first raise the feet upward and then raise the head and chest. Push the feet backwards and downwards. Look up. Breathe normally. The body will rock on the abdomen because of breathing. Feel the pressure. Hold it till the count of four breaths. Exhale and release the feet and bring your hands to the sides of the body. Breathe normally. Repeat once the body has settled.

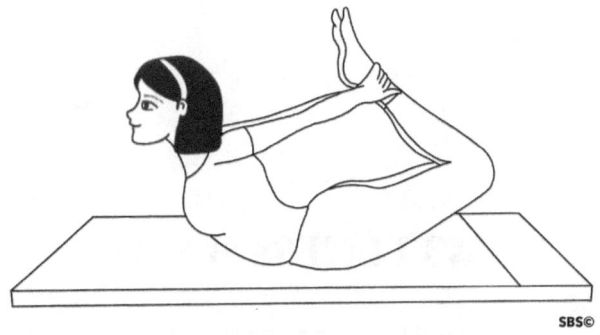

Figure 34. Full bending of spine.

Rest position

Keep the palm of your left hand on the floor. Cover it with your right palm. Keep your chin over the palms. Relax the whole body. Listen to your heartbeat. Breathe normally. Turn the body on your right side and sit up.

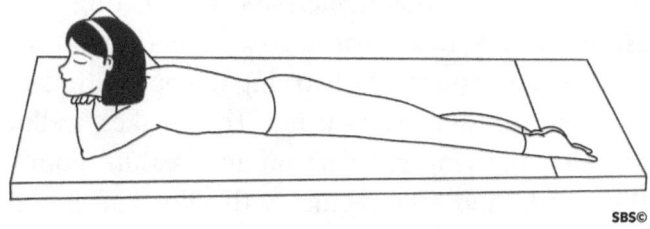

Figure 35. Rest position

Sit in chin mudra

Feel the effect of these exercises on your body and mind. It is beneficial to do pranayama, followed by visualization. Thereafter, express gratitude, as discussed in the chapter 'Way to Pranic Wellness'. It takes about 45 minutes to do all these.

WELLNESS BATH

Bathing is therapeutic

Routine bath is for cleaning the body and refreshing the mind. Wellness bath is more than that. It is diagnostic, therapeutic and meditative. It is done as a ritual, in a particular sequence, while being watchful of all activities being done for bathing. Gently press the whole body to feel any pain and stiffness, to identify any innocuous tenderness, so that timely corrective measures are taken to treat it. It will be a revelation for you to see where all your body is trying to cope with the pressure which your lifestyle is causing. This makes wellness bath diagnostic. Applying pressure on acupressure points located in the hands and feet regulates the flow of energy to the corresponding organs. Massaging the marma areas of the body helps regulate life force. There is better blood flow and movement of the lymph. This is the therapeutic contribution of the wellness bath. Watch the movement of your hands on the body, feel the touch and pressure on the different parts of the body and observe the water flowing on your body. This makes the wellness bath meditative. It takes five–ten minutes longer than the routine bath. However, its benefits outweigh the time spent on this bath.

Acupressure Points

There are certain areas in our hands and feet which regulate the flow of energy to the internal organs. These are like switches for regulating the flow of prana. These are activated by pressure. Hence, they are called acupressure points. Figures 36–39 show the internal organs that get stimulated by pressing certain points on the hands and feet. You do not have to remember these details. Just press these areas while bathing.

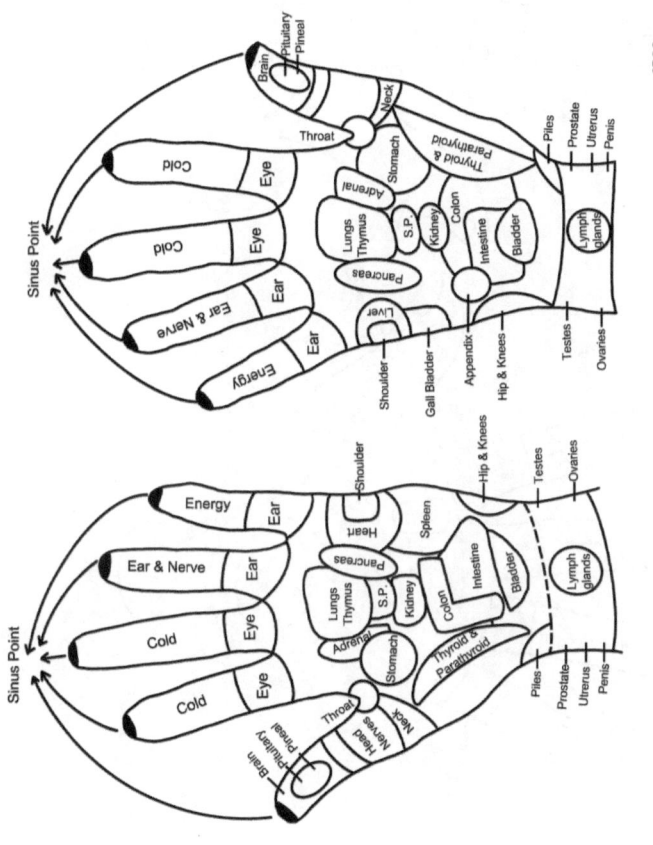

Figure 36. Acupressure points on the left and right palms.

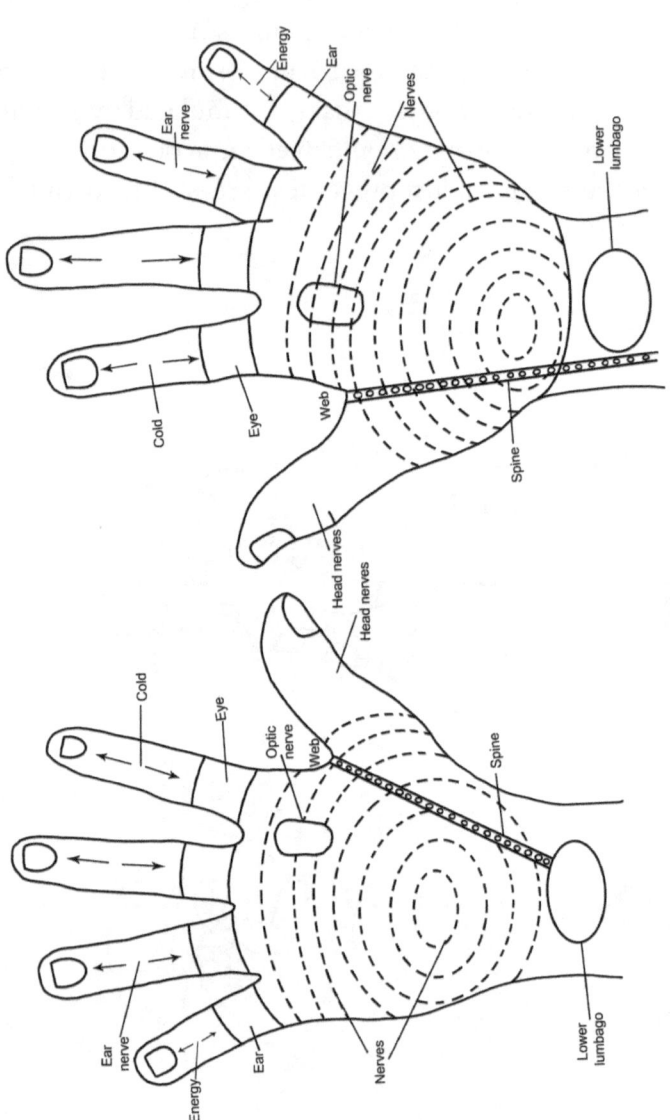

Figure 37. Acupressure points on the back of left and right hands.

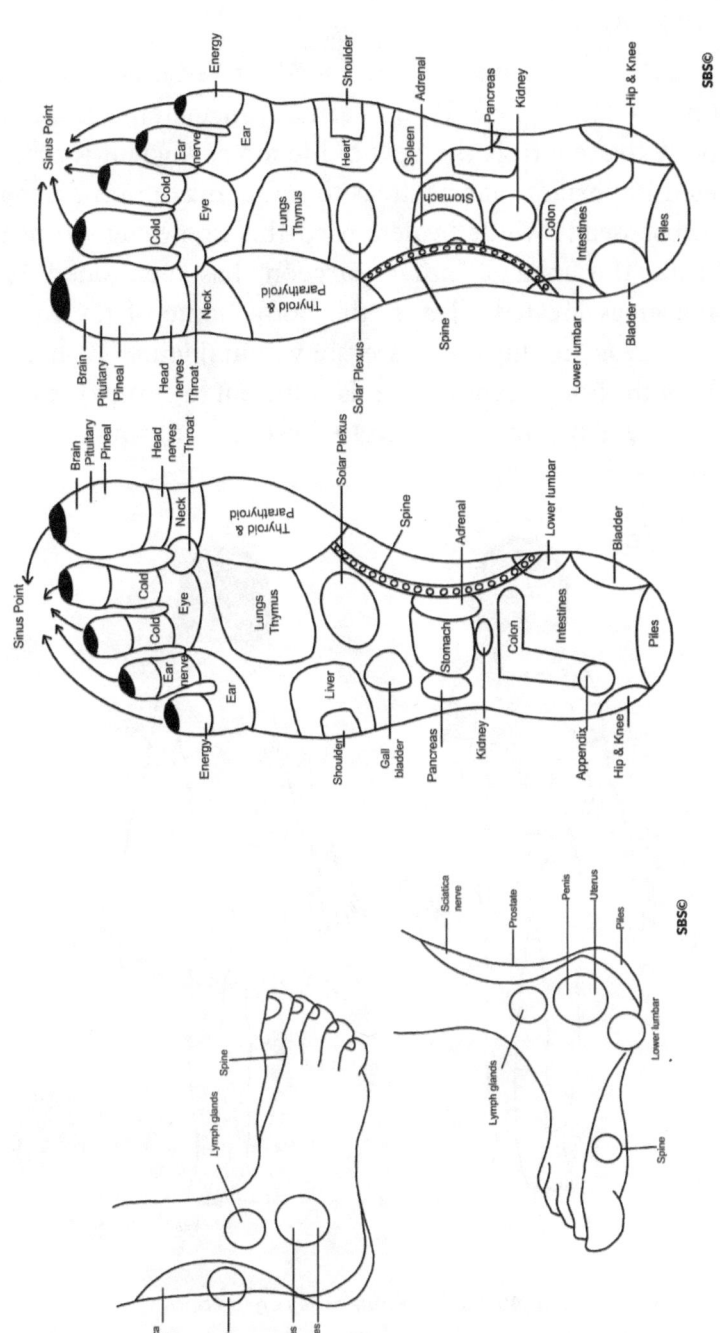

Figure 38. Acupressure points on left and right soles.

Figure 39. Acupressure points in areas around ankle.

Marma Areas

The science of marma was developed by Vedic healers. It is documented in *Atharva Veda*. Marma is an anatomical area in the body that controls the flow of life force. Ancient warriors targeted important marma areas to inflict maximum damage and cause death. Vedic healers used this knowledge to heal. Sushruta, the ancient Indian surgeon, has mentioned 107 marma areas located all over the body. Some of the major marma areas in the body are shown in Figure 40 below. Rubbing the body in these areas is sufficient to ensure the flow of life force. Pay more attention to these areas during bathing.

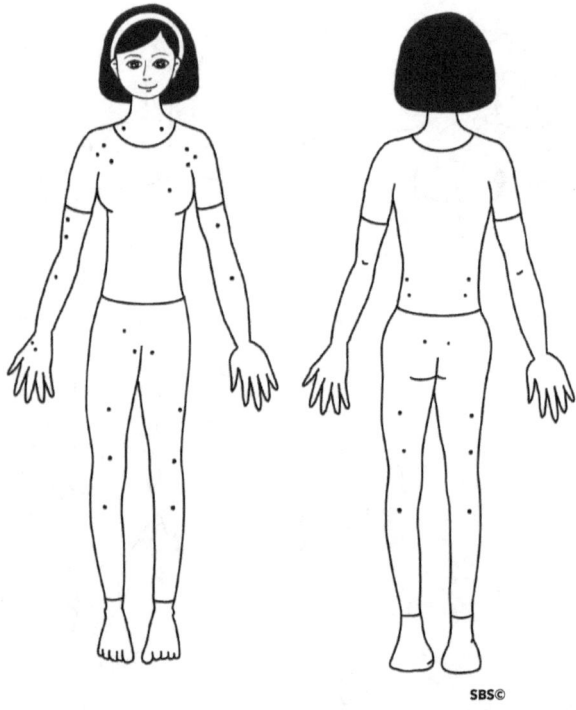

Figure 40. Major marma areas on the body

Bathing Ritual

Take bath in tepid water, which means the water should be neither hot nor cold. Ideally the temperature of water should be 37 degrees Celsius because that is the normal temperature of the body. One can use warmer water in winters and cooler in summers. Extremely hot water removes natural oils from the body and must be avoided. Similarly, extremely cold water can cause cold, sore throat and some other discomforts.

Take bath at the same time every day. Sit on a stool or floor. Use an anti-skid mat to avoid falls in the bathroom. Keep soap, oil, bucket, mug and anything else you need near you. Pour water first on your feet, then the legs, abdomen, chest and finally the head to gradually wet the body. Bathe the body in three segments—the upper body, lower body and the neck and head. Be judicious and innovative to modify the bath rituals as per your body and resources.

Upper Body

Apply soap on the arms, chest, abdomen and back. Take liberal amount of oil on lathered palms and smear it on the upper body. Rub oil and soap on the arms, joints of the wrist, elbow and shoulder. Press and rub fingers, the web between the fingers and back of the hands. Rub more where there are aches. Rub deeply between the thumb and web of the forefinger. Deeply press the whole of the palm with your thumb.

Vigorously press and rub the muscles of the chest to ease out any tenderness. Use the alternate hand to rub the sides of the upper body— the right hand for the left side and the left hand for the right side. Use circular motions on the abdomen, starting from left to right. Be gentle while rubbing the abdomen. Clean the navel. Try and reach the back with your hands as much as possible or use a long handle brush. Rub the sides of the backbone with knuckles of fisted hands as shown in Figure 41. Wash off oil and soap.

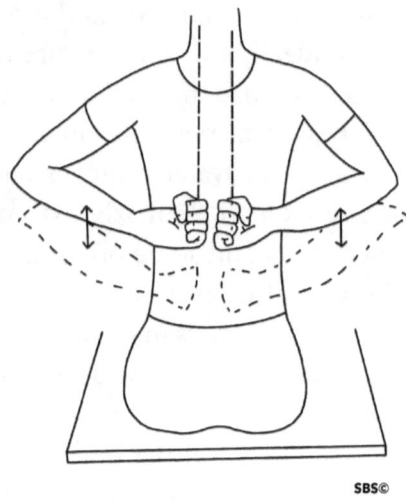

Figure 41. Areas on both sides of spine.

Lower Body

Apply soap on the feet, legs, groin and hips. Apply oil on all these areas. Knead the sole of the left foot up to the toes with your hands. Pinch and press the web between toes. Rub the upper part of the foot up and down. Massage your toes and joints. Rub both sides behind the ankles as shown in Figure 42.

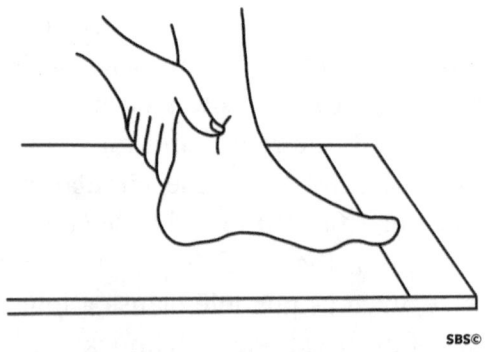

Figure 42. Area behind ankles.

Bend the left leg at the knee. Rub the lower leg with both hands, applying firm pressure on the front and back of the leg while doing upward and downward movements. Straighten the leg and massage the muscles all around the knee. Move the kneecap in clockwise and anticlockwise direction two–three times. Massage the front and back of the upper leg with both hands, in an upward and downward movement and diagonal movement across the leg. Repeat the process on the other leg. Press and rub the pubic and groin areas. Be gentle on the groin area.

Now stand up. With fisted hands, knead the hips one by one. Apply deep pressure in a circular motion where the head of the leg bone joins the pelvis. Rub the tail bone area with both your palms as shown in Figure 43. Sit down and wash off the oil and soap thoroughly.

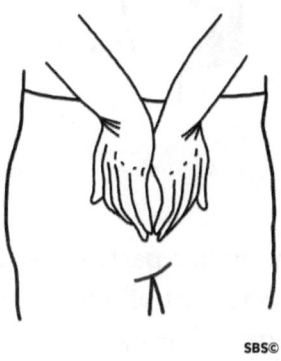

Figure 43. Tail bone area

Neck and Head

Lather up the hands, and take oil on your palms. Now apply the mixture to your neck and face. You must close your eyes while applying soap on your face. Rub the front of the neck starting from the bottom, gently moving upwards. Rub the sides of the neck. Rub the back of the neck in the centre to stimulate the spine. Rub the lower jaw, especially at the angle of the jaw and around the lips. The pent-up emotions get accumulated in this area. This is an animalistic instinct because animals attack by jaws only. Rubbing it will release any accumulated violence. Gently rub your cheeks and forehead. Rub the area in the centre of the eyes in a clockwise direction with fingers of the right hand. This will activate the *agya chakra* located in this area. Press the temple using your fingers. Any tenderness in this area is a sign of stress. Rubbing and pressing it in clockwise and anticlockwise direction will ease the stress. Rub the area around both ears as shown in Figure 44. Pull the ears up and down.

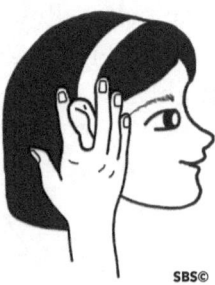

Figure 44. Area around ears

Now gently press the upper part of the eye socket (not the eyes) and then the lower part of it as shown in Figure 45. Do not rub the inner corner of the eyes and upper part of the nose as that stimulates sneezing and watering of eyes.

Figure 45. Area around eyes

Rub the top of the head in the clockwise direction with fingertips of the right hand. This will stimulate the *sahasrara chakra* located in this area. Wash off soap and oil from the neck and head.

Spinal Stimulation

If you shower, allow water from it to run on your backbone for a minute or so. Feel the water falling on the nape and travelling all along your spine right up to the tail bone. It stimulates all the nerves originating from the spinal cord. Else use a mug to direct the flow of water on the spine. Hold it in both hands over your head and drop a thin stream of water on your spine in a slow and steady flow.

Gently moisturize the external ears with the tip of your index finger, but avoid the ear canal. Moisturize the nostrils. Apply moisturiser in the navel with the tip of your little finger. Dry your body with a coarse towel. Rub vigorously as that also stimulates the body. Dry the ear canals with the corners of your towel.

Feel the Freshness of a Bath

Close your eyes. Feel the negativity, stress and disease being washed off. Fold your hands and say a prayer seeking health and happiness, and feel it being bestowed upon you. Then leave the bathing area with gratitude to God and to yourself.

Types of Baths

Oil and Soap Bath

Oil and soap are used in combination, as has been described above. Use any oil or different oils on different days.

Milk and Curd Bath

Using milk and curd to bathe can be very beneficial as both have deep cleaning properties and act as probiotics for the skin biome.

Scrub Bath

Use only water and coarse hand towel to scrub the body clean. Do not scrub too hard. Be gentle. Use a scrub brush or scrub gloves as convenient. You must apply oil or moisturiser on the body after this bath. This bath exfoliates the skin and enhances the skin biome.

Oil Bath

It is an oil soaking bath and can be done once a month or once a fortnight. Apply oil three times on the body. First application will need more oil. Rub oil vigorously on the whole body. Use circular motion on all joints and to and fro motion on other parts of the body. Apply oil second time and rub again. It will take lesser amount of oil. Then apply oil for the third time and again rub it well on the body. It will take the least amount of oil. By this time your body will be totally drenched in oil. Wait for 10 minutes, and let the oil seep deep into the skin. During this period, sit in a relaxed manner with hands on your knees. Become aware of your breathing and listen to your heartbeat. Wash your body after 10 minutes. Use soap only once so that a thin film of oil remains on the skin. Take precautions in cold weather.

Sun Bath

Drink one–two glasses of water. Sit in sunlight for 10 minutes. Keep the skin as bare as possible. Protect your face and neck with sunscreen lotion. Any time of the day is suitable, but avoid the scorching heat of the Sun. Wash the body immediately and moisturize.

Shower Bath

It is a quick bath for relieving tiredness. It refreshes the mind from negative influences of crowded areas and of any sorrowful event. Stand or sit under a shower or pour water on the body for a minute or so and feel the water flowing on the body. Dry the body. One can take it any time of the day as and when one feels like.

Avoid any type of bath at least for one hour after any meal. It will interfere with the digestive process. The blood from digestive organs will rush towards the skin.

Body Massage

Massage enhances the physical appearance of the body and minimises the effects of ageing. Massage relieves aches, regenerates tissue and corrects internal malfunction. Stimulating the outer surface of the body also stimulates the internal layers and helps move lymph, increase blood supply and re-channelize energy flow. It relaxes the mind and calms you down when you are experiencing heavy emotions. If you have been taking the wellness bath as described above, then you may not require massage as much.

You may massage yourself or get it done by a trained person. The spine and upper back cannot be massaged by oneself. A long-handled brush may be used for the same. Self-massage is not as relaxing as a massage done by someone else, but it is more healing as the pain and tenderness will guide you to be gentle in some parts and go deep in some stiff parts of the body. Also, self-massage is a good exercise which increases circulation and tones up the muscles. Make it meditative by watching all actions that you will be doing while massaging yourself or while someone else is doing it to you. Be in the moment. Avoid listening to music, unless it is a meditative one, and do not engage in any conversation with the masseur.

The procedure and steps are the same as that of a wellness bath. Do not wet the body with water when massaging. Instead, apply warm oil on the body, and rub it in the same way as in wellness bath. Start from the sole of your feet, gradually coming up and finishing at the top of the head. After the massage, wrap your body in a cotton sheet for 20 minutes. Take bath with tepid water. Do not use too much soap. Leave a bit of oil on the body.

Body Packs

In Naturopathy, body packs are used to mildly stimulate the outer area around the eyes, throat and abdomen. The superficial stimulation activates the corresponding deeper layers and internal organs. An eye pack and abdomen pack may be used by everybody. A throat pack is for those suffering from thyroid insufficiency. These packs can be used daily at home by yourself.

Take small towels, one for each eye and the throat (not required if thyroid is normal). Use a medium towel for the abdomen. Wet all these in water and wring the excess water to avoid dripping. Lie down comfortably on a mat. Place the small towels on your eyes and throat and the medium one on the abdomen. Gently cover the eyes, but do not press your eyeballs. The towel on the throat should cover the thyroid gland located on the voice box of the throat. The abdomen should be covered from the sternum to the pubic protuberance. Cover the pack on the abdomen with a dry cloth. Relax for 10–15 minutes. Then remove all the packs.

Be mindful of your breathing during the period of relaxation. Feel the coolness. This will give you a practice for watchfulness. It is so meditative that sometimes you may doze off, which is perfectly fine.

WELLNESS EATING

Dietary indiscretions weaken your vitality

Eating gives us pleasure. Wellness eating is a way to prolong this pleasure before, during and after eating. Every time we have a meal, we get an opportunity to enhance or undermine our health. Wellness eating is about understanding the art of partaking food.

Why to Eat?

Animals eat to fill their stomach, but humans eat to enjoy the food. Humans have three types of hunger— physical, mental and emotional. Physical hunger is quite evident, because there is rumbling of the empty stomach, some may have mild headache or feel low on energy. It is the body's mechanism of communicating that it wants food. One experiences mental hunger either around one's routine mealtime or when craving for a particular food or flavour. Emotional hunger results from emotional distress, unhappiness and wanting to derive happiness out of food. It is an infantile conditioning that gets developed when the child is breastfed by the mother because the child is crying in distress. A connection develops between food and love. Thus, food becomes a substitute for love later in life. This is why people tend to overeat when experiencing mood swings.

The only reason to eat food should be physical hunger. Physical hunger releases a great deal of gastric juices, which enable digestion. If you eat for other reasons, you are overfeeding yourself.

Seventy per cent of sickness is diet-related. Minor changes in eating habits can lead to major changes in health. There are only a few ailments that these changes cannot help prevent, cure or make bearable.

Medical science has drawn attention to the role of inflammaging in wellness. Inflammaging is a low level of inflammation over an extended period of time. It is a little known yet common health condition that speeds up ageing and contributes to an array of diseases like diabetes, arthritis, Alzheimer's and cardiovascular diseases. Over-nutrition, altered gut biome and chronic stress are key factors that contribute to inflammaging. So, eat only when you experience physical hunger. This way you will reduce one of the three main causes of inflammaging.

When to Eat?

The need to eat food is regulated by two centres in the brain—the centre for appetite and centre for satiety. The centre for appetite stimulates hunger and the centre for satiety guides us when to stop eating. The mind can override the command of both the centres. So, we eat when not hungry and we go on eating beyond the feeling of satiety. As a result, with the passage of time both the centres become dormant so we do whatever we want to do with our eating habits. Look out for signals from both centres to control your eating. Eat when your body gives a signal and not when your mind, emotions, sight of food, time for food or friends ask you to do it. Do not indulge in sensual eating. This can only be practised if you have learnt watchfulness, as it will make you aware and enable you to discern whether the signal for food is physical or sensual.

Frequency of taking meals is very subjective. Some persons eat very frequently and digest well. Some persons eat twice or thrice a day and if they eat frequently then they do not digest the food that well. One major meal takes six–eight hours for complete digestion. This meal must get digested before you eat again. It is a healthy practice to keep a gap of 13 hours between the last meal of the day and the first meal of the next day. A small biscuit with morning tea or a fruit make a good pre-breakfast meal if you feel hungry.

Skipping breakfast is not a good practice unless you are not hungry, which means the dinner has not been digested by then. Breakfast kickstarts the metabolic process as it slows down in the night. This awakening of the metabolic process will give you energy for the morning. An empty stomach in the morning produces acid, which causes gas and rumbling. This diminishes the feeling of wellness.

A regulated eating pattern will slowly become a habit that will, by and large, coincide with your hunger signals. Persons on medication should coordinate their mealtime in consultation with their physicians.

When Not to Eat?

In between Meals

The food from previous meal is still being processed in your stomach. Eating before it gets out of your stomach interferes with that process. If you cannot resist, then keep the quantity of snacks to the minimum. Fruits are a good snack as they get easily digested, but limit your intake to only one type of fresh fruit. If you had a heavy breakfast, then wait for at least four hours before snacking of any kind. A light lunch permits you a small snack at teatime, but it should be taken at least two to three hours after lunch. Do not eat snacks immediately before the main meal, whether lunch or dinner. If it is inevitable then, reduce the quantity of the main meal.

When you are too Famished

Drink a glass of water and eat food a few minutes later. Otherwise, you are likely to overeat.

Acute Sickness

The appetite goes down because vital energy of the body gets used in fighting the disease, clearing the toxins and eliminating the dead cells of the body. It is a natural phenomenon of the body, so you should not load it with food which needs energy for digestion. One must limit consumption during sickness. Consume more liquids and easily digestible food during acute illness. Gradually return to normal food once this phase is over.

When in Physical or Emotional Distress:

When you are tired, disturbed, angry, anxious, overwhelmed or sad, the body is not ready to digest food. Digestion gets compromised due to secretion of stress hormones. The state of mind also affects how you perceive the taste, smell and sight of food, which in turn affects the digestive process. It is better to relax and then eat.

What to Eat and Avoid?

Food affects your state of mind. Thus, it is essential that one practises caution and makes informed food choices.

Food is broadly grouped into three types. Some foods increase vitality, energy, health and joy. These include all grains, pulses, nuts, seeds, vegetables, fruits, natural sweeteners like honey, molasses and dairy products (in small quantities). Eat more of these. The second type includes foods that overstimulate, create physical and mental stress. These include onion, garlic, radish, coffee, tea, all stimulants, white sugar, soft drinks, pungent spices, excessively hot, bitter, salty and sour foods. Use these in moderation. The third type includes foods that make a person feel tired and lethargic. These are meat, fish, eggs, paneer, desi ghee (clarified butter) and alcohol. Reduce these as much as you can.

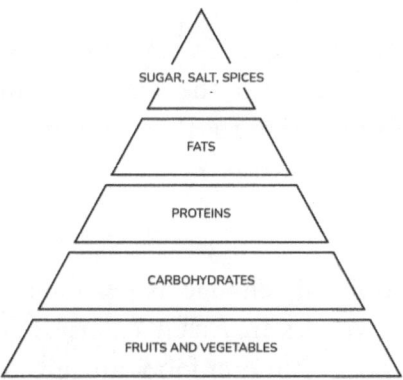

Figure 46. Food pyramid

As shown in Figure 46, fruits and vegetables should form the bulk of your diet. Increase their quantity to reduce carbohydrates from grains. Fifty-five per cent of your food should be from fruits and grains; 20 per cent should come from proteins; 20 percent from oils, seeds and nuts; and only 5 per cent from spices, salt and sugar.

Eat variety of foods so that you can get all nutrients as well as flavours. Variety stimulates more saliva and gastric juices. It also makes available all the vitamins and minerals essential for a balanced nutrition.

Eat Tasteful and Pleasant Foods

Taste, aroma and look are the only sensations that the body understands, and the mind appreciates. While a major part of the food we eat is salty in taste, we also need sour, bitter and pungent-tasting foods like curd, bitter gourd, ginger and pickles respectively, but these must be had in little quantity. Similarly, we should have sweets in small portions because the body converts all tastes to sweet in the mouth. These tastes signal every cell to assimilate variety of foods. If the food does not taste good, it is better not to eat it.

Eat Local

Consume the food produced in your region. The environment in which you live is also the environment in which the vegetation has grown. There is, thus, a natural synergy between you and the local produce.

Eat Seasonal

Foods produced locally change as per the season. The foods that are eaten in winters are rich in calorie, high in energy and keep the body warm. Summer foods are not as calorie-rich but have more water in order to keep the body hydrated and cool. Eating food of one season in other season will inimically affect your health.

Observe Transition of Seasons

Seasons do not change abruptly without a transition period. For instance, in India there are two major shifts from winter to summer and vice-versa. It is advisable to give rest to the body during the transition so that the body can acclimatise itself accordingly. Shift to non-grain foods like flour of '*singhara*' (water caltrop), '*kuttu*' (buckwheat), '*rajgira*' (amaranth) and '*samak*' rice. Eat more vegetables and fruits. Abstain from onions and garlic. Reduce salt and spices. In April, before the intense heat of summer sets in, this transition for nine days is observed. Similarly, in October, before winter sets in, another transition period is observed. During the rainy season, reduce consumption of fruits and vegetables with high water content like cucumber, watermelon and melon. Also, the quality of drinking water is likely to be compromised. It is advisable to drink black cardamom infused water. Add two black cardamom pods in two litres of water. Boil till the colour of water takes the hue of cardamom. Cool it and store in glass bottles. This water is great for boosting immunity and protecting against, the two common ailments in rainy season— common cold and gastric disturbances.

Eat Natural and Fresh

All preserved, canned and tinned foods have additives which are harmful to the body. Industrially modified foods like cornflakes, etc., have the least nutritive value because of the presence of hidden sugars, salts and preservatives. These must be avoided.

Eat Essential Foods

An average adult requires 60 g of proteins, 30 g of fats, 70 mg of vitamin C and two tablespoons of curd spread over the day. Of the 30 g fat, use 20g fat for cooking food using desi ghee (clarified butter), virgin coconut oil, virgin olive oil or virgin sesame oil, and the remaining 10 g can be added to cooked food. Take vitamin C from natural sources, preferably with all major meals because vitamin C is not stored in the body. A fruit or lemon water in the morning, a piece of pickle or a table spoon of amla chutney with lunch and dinner is sufficient. Squeeze half a lemon in soup. Lemon rind has more vitamin C than lemon juice. You can also keep lemon in freezer for 10 hours and grate it on soups and foods as seasoning.

Do not Eat Essential Foods in Excess

If we eat more proteins and fats than what we require, the body does not use it as essential foods but burns it to provide energy. In the process, it leaves certain residues as by-products, which burden the excretory system of the body. It is a waste of money and food to eat large amounts of proteins and fats.

Eat what Suits your Body

What we eat is less important than what we digest. Observe what you eat and how it gets digested. Make a mental note over a period and drop those foods which do not go well with your body. Consult your physician for ordering a food intolerance test, for more precise management of what does not suit you.

Eat as per your Digestive Fire and Metabolism

Both differ from person to person. It is important to read your system well and plan your meals accordingly.

Balanced metabolism

It is indicated by good regular appetite. Digestion feels comfortable with no gas, constipation or bloating. Bowel movements are regular. Such a person digests reasonable quantity and quality of food in all seasons. These people are generally calm, quiet, loving, have great awareness and abundant energy.

Irregular metabolism

It is indicated by a fluctuating appetite. Such persons do not digest food properly, which causes gas, constipation, bloating, pain and diarrhoea. Their skin is dry and joints ache. Such persons also suffer from insomnia and crave fried foods.

Hypermetabolism

It is indicated by an excessive appetite because of which there is excessive eating. This leaves food undigested that causes constipation, gas, bloating, dryness of mouth and heartburn. Such individuals experience intense craving for candies, sweets and chocolates.

Hypometabolism

It is indicated by heaviness in the stomach even when one has not eaten much. This happens when regular diet is not digested properly. Such individuals crave for hot and spicy foods.

Once food is digested in the gut, it gets converted into glucose, amino acids and fatty acids for absorption. These are carried by the blood to the intercellular spaces for utilization by the cells. This aspect is called metabolization. If these are not metabolized by the cells, then either these flow back into the blood or clog the intercellular spaces. Either way, it is harmful. Unutilised glucose combines with haemoglobin and reduces its oxygen carrying capacity. It is excreted through urine. Amino acids and fatty acids get deposited in the body.

Unmetabolized food does not cause disease in a day. There are six stages of disease: accumulation, aggravation, overflow, relocation, manifestation and diversification. Cells take metabolites from the intercellular space. If they cannot, then the unmetabolized food accumulates in the intercellular space. This stage is called accumulation. Cells cannot transport their waste out due to accumulation in the intercellular spaces. Cells get backed up. This is known as aggravation. The disease is still limited to a local area. If this situation is not corrected, then the waste from the cells seeps into the blood, lymph and gastrointestinal tract. This is overflow. The disease is no more localised. It is on the move and relocates to other parts of the body. The next stage is manifestation. The signs and symptoms of a specific disease like diabetes, arthritis, asthma or other organs become apparent. By the time the disease becomes apparent, four stages of derangement have already passed. Once the disease has manifested, it is very difficult to reverse it. The last stage is diversification, when the disease spreads all over the body. The disease is now irreversible. Some factors that could cause the first stage include an unhealthy diet, seasonal change, lifestyle changes and stress. Some initial signs of unmetabolized food include coated tongue, dry mouth, bad breath, pale skin, muscle spasm, generalised body ache, headache, fatigue, uneasiness and confusion. Hence, it is critical that one analyses one's state of health every morning and evening.

Be judicious in combining food

Different foods get digested at different speeds. Some foods get digested easily and leave the stomach early. Some stay in the stomach for longer periods. This mismatch beyond a limit affects the movement of food from the stomach and causes indigestion, fermentation and putrefaction. Fatty foods stay in the stomach longer than protein-rich foods, vegetables and fruits.

Eat bread and butter only as a meal. Combine meat, chicken, fish or paneer with only complex carbohydrates and not refined flour. Also avoid adding vegetables and fruits to such a meal. Do not eat starchy food items like cakes, pastries and puddings with any meals. If you cannot resist, then take the smallest helping, not more than two tablespoons or eat it as a separate food after some time but in the same quantity.

Eat one type of fruit at a time, especially sweet fruits like bananas, mangoes and dates. You may combine two types of fruits with raw vegetables or with steamed vegetables, but keep the carbohydrates from grains to the minimum. Avoid combining fruits with cooked food. Raw food should not be combined with cooked food. Likewise, fresh food and leftovers should also not be combined. Foods cooked together in the same pot, like mixed vegetables, may be eaten. Eating only steamed vegetables or raw vegetables without fats is not advisable because small amount of fat is required to absorb the minerals in vegetables. Drink water 20 minutes before or after the food.

Eat simple because simple meals are easy to digest but do not make the food monotonous. Ensure all the six tastes are present in all the meals. Take one main dish with accompaniments of curd, chutney, pickle, papad and salad in one meal. Eat with either rice or chapatti.

Where to Eat?

While eating food, the life force and mind open and become vulnerable to the environment around. Thus, the ambience of the dining place, the social circumstances and the company of people around you affects your digestion. Eat in a serene, soothing and peaceful place with calm and quiet people where one feels relaxed.

Eat food alone and in silence as far as possible. In Indian households, it was common for the head of the family, who bore all the financial burden, to eat in solitude so that mealtime for that person is peaceful, and food is eaten leisurely. Such a meal becomes therapeutic. It is, thus, a poor eating practice to share your mealtime with the boss! An occasional meal in others' company does not matter because it takes time for the eating environment to manifest on the mind.

How to Eat?

Take a Food Break

Eat only food during that period. Do not even think about the activity that you were performing before the food break. This will help your mind relax. You will get mentally rejuvenated to do any activity better.

Eat Comfortably

Sit in a comfortable position. Eating food while standing and on the go should be avoided. Arrange the food on your plate in a way that the sight and smell of food encourage abundant secretion of gastric juices.

Eat Unhurriedly

Eating in a relaxed manner, slowly and silently, gives you more time to enjoy the flavour and taste. The stomach takes about 20 minutes to activate the centre of satiety. The faster we eat food, the lesser are the chances of activating the centre of satiety. Digestion is insufficient if food is eaten too quickly.

Eat Watchfully

Food tastes better when you are aware of what you are eating. Taste nourishes the mind and mind nourishes the body. Without watchfulness, you only stuff the food in. It neither gives taste nor proper nourishment. Avoid distractions of phone calls or TV while eating. Keep the general conversation to the minimum until the end of meal. Keep aside all problems and difficulties from the mind. Calmness is conducive to digestion. Anger and tension cause indigestion.

Be Meditative

Say a small prayer of gratitude firstly to the creator who created you and your food, secondly to the one who grew food for you, thirdly to the one who prepared this food for you and the one who served it. Now savour the look and aroma of food. All these activities prepare the body and mind to receive food. Start with either bitter or pungent taste as it stimulates all taste buds. End it with a bit of sweet taste as it settles all taste buds. Enjoy your food till the last morsel. Take small bites of food with full awareness. See your hand bringing it to your mouth and putting it in your mouth. Feel the taste of food for a moment and then, with full attention, chew it till you feel that morsel has become liquid or semisolid. Feel the change of texture from solid to semisolid and then swallow it knowingly. Feel it passing down the throat before you pick up the next morsel. Your mind will be engaged in every moment of eating, which will become a meditative practice to give you tranquillity.

Chew Adequately

Non-fried solid foods should be chewed about 30 times and fried foods for a little longer. Protein-rich foods need less chewing but should still be broken into small pieces. While chewing, saliva is secreted and mixed with food. Chewing is adequate when solid food becomes a pasty liquid and the taste of bolus (food that has been chewed and mixed in the mouth with saliva) from the initial bite turns sweet. Sweet taste means the complex carbohydrates have been converted into sugar. Chew the food in your mouth well to start this digestive process before it is further digested in the stomach. Another indication of adequate chewing is a mild tiredness of the jaw muscles. When you chew more, the quantity that you eat will get reduced to half. Chew the food even more when you are sick.

Post Eating Ritual

Once you are done eating, say a prayer of gratitude, and make a wish that the food you have consumed enhances your prana. Follow an old proverb: 'After lunch rest a while, after dinner walk a mile'. After lunch, close your eyes for 20 minutes so that the digestive process does not get disturbed. Walk for some time after having dinner, but ensure that the walk is leisurely and not fast paced as that will interfere with digestion. The aim is to let food go down from the stomach before you hit the bed. Finally, feel the energy and satisfaction of having eaten well.

How Much to Eat?

Stop Eating before you Feel Full

Do not go on eating because the food tastes good. An empty stomach has space equal to the size of both your palms. Irrespective of the food you are eating, it should not exceed the quantity that fills up your palms held together. Since your palms are so unique to you, the quantity of food that you will eat will be different from others.

Stop Eating when you are Still a Bit Hungry

You may feel that you can and need to eat a little more but that feeling will subside when you leave the meal area. As a principle take small helpings initially so that you can reduce wastage if you are unable to consume it. It is normal to insist on guests to take another helping of food but to yield or not to yield is your choice. There are no hard and fast rules as to how you decline without offending the host. One way is to take a small helping initially so that you can oblige the host later.

Fill Up only Two-thirds of the Stomach

An empty stomach has some air, which gets displaced as we eat food. When the stomach is half-filled with food, the displaced air is released as a burp. The first burp is an indication that sufficient food has been eaten. It is advised that one should not eat any more solids after this green signal, and fill up the balance with liquids alone. If you do not stop at the first burp, then your body receives a yellow signal in the form of a second burp. If you still go on eating, then the third burp is a red signal that you must stop. Any more food is a violation which will invite penalty. Digestion slows down if the quantity of food is too much. The body has an innate capacity to convert food to the substances that it needs, provided it is not overloaded. That is why eating a bit less is healthier and never leads to undernourishment or malnourishment.

Eating one large meal and not dividing the food into three different times is unhealthy.

Fasting

Fasting is the first approach to get rid of unmetabolised food. We all love a weekly off, a day of rest on a Sunday. We also go on vacation for a change of taste, for relaxation and rejuvenation.

Similarly, give an off to your digestive system too. You will feel abundantly energetic and experience a sense of lightness and peace. We suggest that you go hungry once in a while.

Miss a meal once a week. Have a bowl of khichri or very light dinner on Sunday. Skip your regular breakfast and take a small bowl of one fruit instead. Have a light lunch of steamed vegetables. You can also opt for a liquid diet and consume juices, soups, lassi, milk, tea, etc. during breakfast and lunch. Have light dinner comprising dal, chapatti and vegetables.

Take only fruits and vegetables in one meal for two days in a week. This way you will not starve and crave for food during fasting. Starving and craving is detrimental to wellness.

In addition to taking the load off your system, fasting also helps you understand hunger differently. It allows you to test your willpower to not think of food. It enables you to become aware of something within you that is watching your hunger and willpower. This viewer is the soul. You will dwell in your soul because of fasting. That is why fasting is translated as '*upvaas*' in Sanskrit, where '*up*' means 'subordinate' and '*vaas*' means 'to live'. You live as a subordinate to your soul.

Intermittent fasting has proven to be effective in reducing inflammaging. This should be done twice a week for six months for best results. Keep a window of eight hours for moderate eating. The remaining 16 hours (8 o'clock in the evening to 12 o'clock in the noon the next day) should be kept aside for fasting. During the fasting period, consume only low-calorie fluids to maintain water in the body. During the rest of the eight hours, eat low calorie and easily digestible food in small quantities.

WELLNESS DRINKING

Water is elixir

The spiritually inclined statement by the mystic, Rahim, '*bin paani sab soon*', meaning 'nothing shines without water' is scientifically proven. The human body comprises 70 per cent water and cannot function in its absence. Staying well hydrated is so critical for the blood, lymph and skin that water balance is very delicately monitored by the thirst centre in the body. This centre is located in the hypothalamus. It gets activated by as little as one per cent change in the water balance in the body.

How to Recognize Water Imbalance?

Thirst is an obvious indication. The saliva becomes thick, because of which there is bad odour from the mouth. Dry tongue, dry lips and dry skin indicate water insufficiency in the body. Scanty and dark coloured urine is also a warning that the quantity of fluids consumed is less.

How is Water Lost?

Breathing, digestion, sweating, urination, pooping and exposure of skin to the air cause water loss. These are essential physiological functions and cannot be moderated to retain water in the body. Hence, water must be replenished from time to time.

How to Replenish Water?

Wellness drinking is an important aspect of nutrition, especially in the elderly. The thirst centre is less responsive in older persons, so they should not wait for a thirst signal. Instead, they should consume fluids from time to time.

Aging also slows down the ability of your gut to absorb water. As one advances in age, what one drinks is even more important than what one eats.

Plain water does quench thirst, but it does not adequately replenish water in the cells. Robert K. Crane discovered that the body's cells used sodium and glucose for transporting water across the cell wall. Drinking water with some salt and sugar in it is more beneficial than plain water. Lemon water with a pinch of salt and half teaspoon of sugar is the cheapest and best drink for maintaining water balance.

It is our personal experience that drinking tea quenches thirst better than drinking plain water even in summer seasons. Drink tea more often. Drink soups and juices instead of plain water.

Water, by itself, does not stay in the gut for a long time. A glass of water taken will be filtered out as urine in no time. If water is taken through vegetables and fruits, then it gets absorbed in the gut. Fibres from vegetables and fruits stay in the gut for sufficient time. So, the water retained in these fibres becomes available for gradual absorption. When it is absorbed slowly in the gut only then it becomes available to the cells. Drinking vegetable soups and juices is, thus, more beneficial. Non-vegetarian soups do not give this advantage. Drink vegetable juices like bottle gourd, aloe vera, ash gourd, coriander and wheatgrass. If feasible drink vegetable juice two-three times a day. At one time the soup should not be more than 200 ml, and juice not more than 50–100 ml. Avoid canned juices and readymade soups. Instead, prefer having fresh home-made juices and soups.

Fruit juices should be avoided as they have the tendency to raise the blood sugar. Consume whole fruits instead as that will give you more fibre. Berries, citrus fruits and melons are rich in water.

In addition to the above measures, take sips of water at normal temperature and slightly warm in winters to stay well hydrated in between meals.

Drink at least two–three litres of fluid, in divided quantities, in a day. Stay well hydrated, especially while exercising, and when out in the open and under the Sun.

Drink half a glass of water or a cup of soup about 5 minutes before your meal. It will aid in better secretion of saliva and gastric juices. Drink 100 ml herbal butter milk (lassi) after lunch and dinner instead of plain water. Plain water will move from stomach faster than food and may affect digestion. Hence, avoid drinking too much water immediately after a meal.

Drinks that contain more than 10 per cent of alcohol cause dehydration. They deplete water. Most wines, whiskies, beer and other forms of alcohol fall in this category. Be cautious in consuming alcoholic beverages. Consume more fluids, if you are enjoying an alcoholic drink, to avoid hangover.

Drink plain water as per your thirst, but avoid overdoing it as that will deplete the salts in your body through urine. Clear urine, like water, is an indication that you have consumed more water than you need.

WELLNESS BIOME

Symbiosis protects

Biome refers to a group of virus, bacteria, bacteriophage, protozoa and fungi that live in your gut and on skin. The biome weighs about one– two kg. Your body harbours more than 100 trillion microorganisms. You are not aware of these because they are not visible to the naked eye. Your biome comes from your parents and your environment. It lives on you. It survives because you give it food and shelter. In return, it contributes to your health. This symbiotic relation is very critical for your wellness throughout life.

How the Biome Affects Wellness?

The biome keeps you healthy. It helps to digest food, regulate the immune system, produce vitamins and many other substances. A disturbance in the biome is one of the causes of inflammaging.

Some bacteria in the gut produce TMAO[1] from animal foods. TMAO can cause blocked arteries, leading to heart attacks and strokes. That is why a vegetarian diet is healthier.

---

[1] (Tri methylamine N-oxide)

The biome is the first line of defense that protects you from other harmful bacteria. The disease-causing microorganisms are all around us and also live within the biome. These cause disease only when the biome becomes weak and the disease-causing microorganisms multiply.

The microbes of skin and gut communicate with each other and with the nervous system. That is why if you are mentally disturbed, the stomach and skin also get affected and vice-versa.

How to Maintain the Biome?

Your wellness keeps the biome healthy. In general, managing stress, exercising regularly, getting enough sleep, avoiding trigger foods, avoiding smoking and limiting the use of alcohol keeps the biome healthy. Limiting the intake of sugar, artificial sweeteners and refined carbohydrates can also help as such foods help in the growth of unhealthy bacteria. Antibiotics and antiseptics kill microbes. Use them only under medical supervision.

Prebiotics, probiotics and postbiotics are three types of foods that help in maintaining the biome.

Prebiotics

These are foods that help the biome grow. Diverse range of plant-based foods such as legumes, beans, fruits, vegetables, whole grains, flax seeds, wheat bran, red wine, green tea, dark chocolates and olive oil are all prebiotics. Increase the consumption of these and reduce the foods from animal origin.

Probiotics

These foods help in restoring the biome. Fermented foods, like curd, yoghurt, kanji, idli, *kimchi, baasi roti*, sourkraut, sourdough, kefir, etc., are natural resources of biome. Some persons do not like the taste of these foods; they can take probiotic supplements for replenishing, but only as per the advice of their doctor.

Postbiotics

Some substances are produced by the biome in the process of multiplying while digesting your food. Short chain fatty acids that lubricate the stools are one of them. Postbiotics are utilized by the skin and gut to maintain their health and further promote the biome.

The skin biome gets enhanced if we wash the dishes, interact with plants, soil and animals. Sweat it out a few times a week. Sweat works as a prebiotic for the microorganisms in the skin. Use topical probiotics, like lassi, curd and yoghurt, on the skin while bathing. Drink six–eight glasses of water per day to keep your skin moist and protect its biome.

Maintain moisture by applying oil and moisturizers which do not harm these microbes.

The skin is acidic and conducive to maintain the biome. Soaps are alkaline and upset this balance. Use soaps sparingly or use biome soaps, natural and neutral soaps to protect the skin biome. After 70 years of age, the skin becomes more acidic, which is likely to disturb the skin biome. An occasional milk bath will restore the biome on the skin.

Do not exfoliate the skin vigorously. Avoid overwashing and over scrubbing. Gently pat and dry the skin. Avoid exposure to harsh Sun, antiperspirants and deodorants as these reduce the microbial population on the skin. Natural deodorants like neem and sandal are better. Use hand sanitisers sparingly as they kill microbes. Avoid synthetic fabrics, especially synthetic undergarments, as they are in direct contact with the skin. Instead, use cotton as that enhances the skin biome.

Biome has attracted lot of research lately, especially after COVID-19. Your biome holds the clue in your fight against viruses.

WELLNESS POOPING

Evacuation dictates digestion

Elimination of the body's wastes is as important as ingestion. The pleasure of effectual defecation needs no elaboration. Ineffectual defecation restricts your creativity and work efficiency. It causes mental restlessness, sadness, depression, loss of appetite, dullness, headache, nausea, bad breath, thickly coated tongue and a general feeling of heaviness and discomfort in the abdomen.

Each person's bowel activity varies—one may do it after every meal, others once a day or at times more than that. Some evacuate twice in the morning with a gap of one hour. Each of these is perfectly healthy if the pattern of evacuation is regular and satisfactory.

Why Ineffectual Defecation?

The primary requirement for evacuation is that the bowels must fill up. A low-roughage diet does not fill up the bowels completely while a high-roughage diet will fill the bowel too often, leading to the urge to evacuate time and again. Moderating the diet in both the cases is the key.

If we are not properly hydrated, the stools become hard,

and this affects defecation. Drink plenty of fluids. Wellness eating and wellness drinking will give proper digestion and lead to natural and satisfactory defecation.

Insufficient defecation is a sign of poor overall wellness. Ineffectual defecation also increases with age because of weak nerves and weak musculature. Once wellness has been restored, the nerves and musculature gain strength. The body settles in a routine. This improves defecation.

Problems of ineffectual evacuation are more mental and emotional than physical. Chronic tension plays a vital role. The most common cause of inefficient defecation is a habit to ignore the natural urge to relieve. You are refusing the body rest from stress because of which it gets conditioned to ignore these natural urges, which leads to constipation and other problems.

What can be Done for Effective Defecation?

Be Meditative and Focused but not Tense

Defecation is a coordinated process of involuntary reflex and voluntary effort of the body to create enough force to remove waste. Evacuation should be unhurried so that one is relaxed physically, mentally and emotionally to finetune and coordinate these two processes. This coordination requires undivided attention to the act of defecation, so that you can become aware of the involuntary reflex. While pooping, avoid reading, listening to music, riddle solving or brooding as these divide your attention.

Establish a Routine

Prepare for evacuation at approximately the same time every day. Drink two-three glasses of warm water before defecation time. Walk around for some time. If there is no urge, do exercises like vertical stretching of the body, sideways stretching and waist twisting two–three times to stimulate the bowels. Please refer to the wellness exercises in this book. In addition, you may squat on the floor if your knees permit, and shift to the pot when the urge builds up.

Naturopathy Advocates Gentle Stimulation of Abdomen to Elicit Gastro-colic Reflex

Keep your right palm on the abdomen below the sternum and move the palm, very gently and slowly, in circular motion from left to right on whole of the abdomen. Use a small piece of soft cloth under the hand if that feels more comfortable. You can also apply oil for easy gliding of the hand. Be mindful of the movement of palm and its feel on the abdomen. This will divert your mind from any tension that is interfering with the natural process of evacuation. Carry out this process while sitting on the pot. It will initiate the gastro-colic reflex and an urge to move the stools. This is the involuntary urge. As you feel this urge, make a simultaneous voluntary effort to evacuate.

Acupressure Therapy

This involves rubbing and applying pressure on the chin with fingers and thumb for one–two minutes as shown in Figure 47.

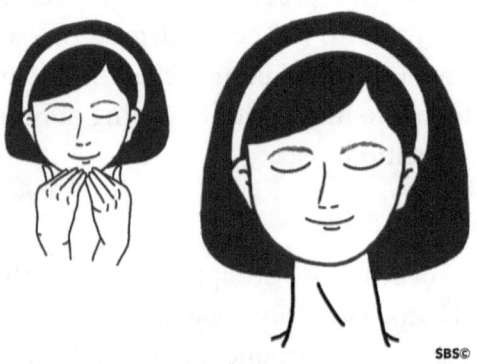

Figure 47. Acupressure area around chin

While doing this, keenly observe the involuntary reflex and coordinate your voluntary effort for smooth evacuation.

Following a routine regularly for a few days will establish bowel movements.

These days we have transitioned to the sitting type of water closets or WCs, instead of the traditional squat toilets. In squatting position, the abdomen would get pressed by the legs. The pressure would help in initiating the involuntary reflex, and the bracing of abdominal muscles would help in the voluntary effort to expel the stools. It is, thus, advisable to use a stool on which you can perch your feet, while using the sitting type of water closet. Some special stools are also available in the market. This will bring the legs near the abdomen as in squatting position and help in evacuation.

Observe your body after defecation. Bring your awareness to the abdominal area and see how much time it takes to return to normal. It takes about 10 minutes for the gastro-colic area to resettle. You may rest for this period if you feel like. Do not consume any liquid or solid food during this period. When food enters the stomach, the body releases a hormone that causes the colon contractions, which may disturb the re-settling of the reflex and may cause ineffectual pooping.

WELLNESS SLEEP

Sleep is solace

Sleep is a natural phenomenon. Every living being must sleep because it helps the body's healing mechanism to function at its best to make new cells and recycle old ones.

Why Disturbed Sleep?

Dreams and disturbed sleep are peculiar to humans. This was not so when humans, like plants and animals, lived in sync with nature. Moreover, now a days it is almost impossible for humans to sleep in the natural surroundings because they are habituated to sleep indoors. In addition, modern houses do not allow sufficient ventilation and exchange of gases for a healthy sleep. The worst scenario is in air- conditioned bedrooms, which control the environment artificially.

The stresses of modern life keep you mentally stimulated even during sleep. It does not allow you to switch off naturally and as instinctively as is the case with animals. This has made sleeplessness a big problem for humans. You go on thinking, planning and scheming the whole day, and it continues even in the sleep as dreams.

A healthy body sleeps less and deeply. How many of us can

claim to be healthy? Quite unfortunately, the number seems to be decreasing, not increasing, despite all medical advances. Good sleep comes when the body and mind are equally tired. Imbalance in either of the two interferes with normal sleep. If you are mentally stimulated, the mind will not let the body sleep even if it is tired. Any physical discomfort will make sleeping difficult.

How to Promote Wellness Sleep?

Sleeping in an open and natural environment is not a possibility anymore. Instead, it may help if you can bring the natural environment to your bedroom. Placing a snake plant, spider plant, jasmine, aloe vera and lavender indoors can be very beneficial. Snake plant and aloe vera emit oxygen during night. Jasmine and lavender have soothing effect on the body and reduce anxiety. Spider plant absorbs odour and chemicals from the room. Alternately, essential oils like lavender, clary sage, frankincense, jasmine, khus (vetiver), etc., can be used in candles, soaps or directly on the earlobes to bring the fragrance of nature inside bedrooms.

Natural remedies for sleep problems are better than medications. A very old remedy is to drink a cup of warm milk just before sleep. You can add a pinch of turmeric, black pepper or nutmeg. Milk has tryptophan, which aids in sleeping. Sleep within 10 minutes of drinking it, because if you stay awake, then tryptophan encourages secretion of serotonin which will give you a feeling of well-being but take away sleep. Chamomile, ginger, cinnamon, rooibos, mint and herbal tea also aid in sleep. Take a cup before you retire for the night.

A tepid water shower or warm foot bath before sleeping warms the whole body and encourages restful sleep. Moisturize the skin after bath, but do not rub the body vigorously as that will take sleep away.

Bhramri and *Anuloma Viloma Pranayama* practised just

before sleeping help calm the mind and induce restful sleep. Please refer to the chapter 'Way to Pranic Wellness' for more details.

You should not place your head towards north while sleeping. This is applicable when you are in the northern hemisphere. In the southern hemisphere the head should not be in the south. The magnetic pull may cause pressure on your brain. Special care must be taken in old age and if the blood vessels are weak, as one may get haemorrhage or paralytic stroke. If you are young and healthy, then this may not happen, but your sleep may get affected due to excessive circulation of blood to the brain. Use a pillow to sleep as it reduces the blood supply to brain when you lie down.

Figure 48. Foot bath

Wellness eating and wellness exercises will aid in sleeping. Take care not to indulge in heavy exercises and games at least two hours before bedtime. Let the body cool down before you hit the bed. Heavy foods like meat, paneer, root vegetables, fats, sugar, coffee, alcohol and chemical stimulants agitate the brain. Take light dinner at least three hours before bedtime if you want to sleep well.

Use your bedroom or your bed only for sleeping. This will condition your mind to sleep.

Sleep Routine

Try to sleep and wake up at the same time as it establishes a rhythm that conditions the body and mind to fall asleep at the usual time. Start preparing for sleep about 20 minutes before sleep time. Gently apply any non-irritating cream or oil to your face and in your nostrils. It reduces dryness of the nasal lining and protects it from viruses.

Examine the Activities of the Day

Sit in a comfortable position in your bed and mentally take a stock of the activities of the day. Reflect on the following:

What you ate and how well it has been digested? Make a note of what food did not go well with you. What were your plans for the day? How much of these has been achieved? What is still pending? Note the pending jobs in your diary for the next day. This will take off the burden of remembering as that can also interfere with sleep.

What thoughts, feelings and emotions crept up during the day's interactions with others? Which of these are lingering on? Take a deep breath and release them. There will be no emotional residue that needs processing during sleep.

Feel a sense of gratitude to those who were helpful towards you. Forgive those who were an obstruction. Forgive yourself also for any infringement that you may have caused to others.

Say a Mental Prayer with Closed Eyes

There is a Christian prayer which says, 'God I took care of the body, mind and soul when I was awake. But since I am going to sleep, I leave all these to your care. Return these to me when I wake up.' This becomes the reason for expressing gratitude to God as the first thing on waking up.

Lie down comfortably in bed in a position that suits you. Avoid any movement during sleep as it indicates some disturbance or imbalance. Now watch your breathing. Observe your breath and its rhythm. Do not change the breathing pattern. You will not know when you have fallen off to sleep. At times you may wake up at night. Keep your eyes shut, and if you find it difficult to fall asleep again, observe your breathing.

Wake up at the same time every day. This will affirm the body clock's sleeping pattern. Do not open your eyes immediately on waking up. Let the twilight zone be the time for silent gratitude to God and the Universe for giving you another day. Rub your hands together to activate all nerve endings. Place your warm palms upon your eyes. Blink your eyes in the darkness of the palms and then open your eyes.

Clench your hands into fists three to four times. Move your wrists and elbow joints, raise your hands up and down. Similarly flex your feet three–four times, move your ankles and knees. Please refer to the chapter 'Wellness Exercises' for more details on minor exercises. Now, turn on the right side of the body and get up. This is ancient wisdom. Plausible reason could be to avoid pressure on the heart if you roll over on the left side to get up. But no scientific study validates this at present.

Examine Activities during Sleep

Sit comfortably in the bed. Reflect on the following:

Feel your energy. Has sleep refreshed you? What kind of thoughts flashed in the twilight zone? On waking up you should feel happy, clear- headed with positive thoughts, optimistic and energetic to start another day. You should be alert without any aches, pains, heaviness in head and abdomen. Your body should feel flexible and not stiff.

Examine the quality of sleep and mentally note the number of times you woke up, felt heaviness in abdomen, passed gas, got out of bed to pass urine, the amount of turning and tossing and the dreams you had. If you have dreamt, then be assured that you have slept.

Now go to the bathroom, and look at your face in the mirror. See how your sleep affects your face. Examine the coating on your tongue, taste, dryness of mouth and feeling of heartburn, if any. Feel how the dinner has been digested. Make a note if it has not gone down well.

Dream

Dreaming shows that the mind has been working. Dreams are the body's way of processing physical or psychological restlessness because of happiness or unhappiness. Dreams are an expression of anything that has not been allowed to express itself at any time, in any life. The subconscious and the unconscious mind of the individual throws up these buried desires when you are not conscious in sleep. This is nature's way to play out your unfulfilled desires to reduce their burden on your mind. In a way, it is a release from your dark side, but sometimes it becomes your nightmare.

Dreams are random pickups from the memory of the mind. Dreams can be very weird and totally unconnected to the present life and, thus, unexplainable. Do not try to find any message or meaning from them.

WELLNESS TALKING

Be soft and slow

༄༅༅

Wellness talking involves regulating what you say and the way you say it. Listed below are a few tips to assist you.

Speak as Little as Possible

Speaking drains physical and mental energy. Conserve your voice and vocabulary by speaking only when absolutely necessary.

Speak Slowly

Slow speaking is mindful speaking. Watch the words coming up in your thoughts. This allows you to weigh them before you speak. You can listen to yourself speaking. You can also judge the reaction of the listener and modify what you are saying. When you speak slowly the listener can also grasp it better, so you are better understood.

When Einstein taught at Princeton, one of his students came to discuss a query. He rattled off the problem to Einstein, who kept quiet and offered no solution. The student looked at him with questioning eyes, to which Einstein replied that he had not understood the problem because of his fast talking and asked him to repeat the problem very slowly. The student complied, and as he finished, Einstein was immediately ready with the solution.

Speak Softly

The softer you speak the more attentive listeners will be. Your words will carry more meaning. All serious issues need to be conveyed softly. It will penetrate the psyche. All meaningful sentiments, like love, are conveyed softly. All violent sentiments are conveyed loudly.

When you speak softly and slowly, it gives the impression of a calm, serene and composed person. This mental makeup helps in wellness. Talking in a shrill and fast-paced voice conveys anxiety, nervousness and tension.

Lower the Tone when Speaking

It improves the quality of speech. Lowering the pitch of voice also stimulates the *vishudhi chakra* located in the neck region. This aspect has been elaborated in the chapter 'Way to Pranic Wellness'.

Silence is Golden

As Mahatma Gandhi rightly said, 'Speak only if it improves upon the silence.' If something can be communicated without words, then prefer to do it that way. Silence saves many a faux pas.

WAY TO PRANIC WELLNESS

Catch the cosmic vibrations

All body-mind activities such as thinking, feeling, breathing, beating of the heart, digestion, evacuation, etc., consume vital energy or prana. Thus, it needs constant replenishment. The body has an innate ability to maintain prana, which can decrease or increase. Prana is neither negative nor positive. It is neutral, but its flow in pranic pathways may be obstructed because of insufficient exchange of gases in the lungs, exchange of metabolites in the cells and exposure to sunlight. If the body does not get adequate metabolites from food, when one is fasting or sick, then the body eats itself to provide these metabolites. It empties its reservoirs. The body goes on living for many days without food, but as the supply dwindles, its vitality and energy levels go on decreasing. If there is no exposure to sunlight, the body will deteriorate despite air, water and food.

How to Optimize Prana?

Food and Prana

The amount of vital energy required to digest food is in direct proportion to the quantity of food consumed. That is why we feel lethargic after eating a heavy meal. Overeating saps energy from our body rather than giving us energy. However, eating small portions at regular intervals keeps one more energetic.

The energy required to digest different foods varies. It takes more energy to digest hot spicy foods, foods rich in calories like dry fruits, fats, animal foods, especially red meat, root vegetables and dairy. We feel more sluggish after consuming these foods because more vital energy is being consumed to process these foods in the body. These foods should be reduced to the minimum as they cannot be avoided altogether. Easily digestible foods give us more energy.

Mind and Prana

Prana is influenced by the state of mind. Kirlian photography has proved that the bioluminescence alters with the change in state of mind. Kirlian also noticed that the bioluminescence alters first and later the physical body becomes unhealthy.

Brooding saps off vital energy. We feel tired even when no physical activity has been done. A state of excitement can also cause a similar effect. That means the way we think has vast influence on our pranic body.

Age and Prana

As age advances, the body's capacity to draw prana diminishes. It will be prudent to change the food habits to reduce the quantity of foods

and eliminate red meat and other foods which one finds difficult to digest or which have been identified to not go well with you. Reduce alcoholic beverages as much as you can; it is better to drop them altogether. Moderate your physical activities also to conserve prana. Wellness breathing and pranayama in combination with Tibetan rites and wellness exercises help regulate prana. These must be practised every day, especially as you advance in age.

WELLNESS BREATHING

Breathing is life

Breathing is an involuntary activity and continues on its own. One rarely notices it or bothers if one is doing it right. Normally, you inhale half a litre of air at a time and exhale the same amount. You can increase it to two litres if you properly expand and contract the chest and abdomen during inhalation and exhalation. Therefore, the correct way of breathing must be learnt, especially by those who lead a sedentary life. The more the lungs expand and contract, the better is the breathing. Wellness breathing is slow and deep as it allows the lungs to fill in more air. It gives more time for the air to stay in the lungs, which improves the exchange of oxygen and carbon dioxide in blood.

Fast and shallow breathing allows only small volumes of air to be inhaled and exhaled. The exchange of gases is insufficient. If you are anxious, tense and inactive, you become prone to take quick shallow breaths which do not give you optimum energy.

How to Learn Wellness Breathing?

Practise Abdominal Breathing

Lie down or sit cross-legged. Keep your spine straight. Relax the whole body. Place one hand on the abdomen near the navel. Breathe in slowly and deeply, and watch your hand moving outwards. Hold your breath for a second. Then exhale slowly and fully. Watch the hand moving inwards. After exhalation, hold your breath for a second. Constantly watch yourself breathing in, holding the breath and breathing out. Practice this 10–20 times.

Practise Chest Breathing

Try not to move the abdomen during this practice. Breathe in slowly while expanding the rib cage. You will not be able to breathe very deeply. At the end of inhalation, hold your breath for a second. Then slowly exhale by contracting the chest. Do not move the abdomen. At the end of exhalation, again hold your breath for a second. Do it 10–20 times. Watch yourself while doing it.

Practise Abdominal and Chest Breathing with Continuous Flow

Inhale slowly and fill the lungs by expanding the abdomen as much as possible, but without straining it. Now inhale more by expanding your chest as much as you can. This is one inhalation. Do it smoothly in one continuous flow to merge abdominal inhalation with the chest inhalation. Hold your breath for a second or two. Then start exhaling. First contract your chest and then your abdomen and exhale as much as you can, but without straining it. Do it in one continuous flow to merge chest exhalation and abdominal exhalation. Hold for a second or two. Practise for five minutes on day one, and gradually increase to 10 minutes in a fortnight. Watch yourself breathing. Travel inwards with the breath going in. Travel out with the breath coming out. Be aware of holding the breath.

Once you have mastered the art, make it a habit to consciously breathe this way for a minute or more, and as many times as you can remember. Find time to practise this while working, sitting in a chair, watching TV or listening to music. This will gradually condition your natural breathing reflexes to become more efficient. You must do it especially when you feel tired or irritated. Wellness breathing improves your watchfulness and makes you calm. It helps enhance your prana and improve your vitality to fight illness.

PRANAYAMA

Expand the dimensions of prana

Pranayama controls the flow of breath in the body and changes the flow of energy in the pranic body. This alters the state of mind and body. Both the mind and body become more sensitive to vibrations in the cosmos and within us. This improves our capability to receive energy from various sources.

Pranayama stops the mind from wandering, reduces thoughts and conflicts. When the mind settles, the soul becomes more active. This is the aim of pranayama. When the soul connects with the source of energy, we realize our oneness. This reveals that our differences are superficial and a result of our ego. This understanding brings tremendous tranquility. Listed below are a few guidelines to help you in the practice of pranayama.

Wear Light and Loose Clothes as per the Weather

The clothes should allow the abdomen to expand during deep inhalations without restricting it. Do not wear belts. Keep the place and time of practice the same for regularity. Practice on empty stomach when the bowels have been moved. Morning is the most suitable time. If practising at other times in the day, ensure that your stomach is empty or do it half an hour before eating.

Sit in Chin Mudra

Keep the body relaxed, especially the facial muscles. Wear a smile on your face for best results. Keep the spine erect but without any strain.

Breathe through your nose unless specified otherwise. No forceful or violent respiration is to be done at any time. That will do more harm than good. Ensure breathing is slow, steady and systematic.

Keep the Mind in Practice

This will enhance watchfulness. Watchfulness is most essential so that you are always aware of the mechanics of pranayama being performed. If you are not watchful, you go on doing pranayama unmindfully which does not give any benefits.

Types of Pranayama

Listed below are some types of pranayama and the techniques to be followed while practising them.

Kapal Bhati Pranayama

Forcefully exhale by contracting the abdominal muscles towards the spine and relax. Inhalation will be automatic once the abdominal muscles are relaxed. Do it in a rhythmic manner with your eyes closed. Watch the movement of the abdomen. Mentally count 25 movements in one session. Be aware of the breath coming out of your nostrils. The counting, and awareness of movement and breath will keep you in the moment and keep the mind involved in the mechanics of *Kapal Bhati*. Once done, open your eyes and feel the effect on your body and mind. Breathe normally during this period.

After three–four breaths, practise the next pranayama.

Anuloma Viloma Pranayama

Maintain chin mudra with the left hand. Fold the index and middle fingers of the right hand, and touch the left nostril with the ring finger and right nostril with the thumb. Keep the right arm at the level of the right shoulder.

Keep the right nostril closed. Breathe in from the left nostril to the count of five. Breathe in very slowly and feel the cool air in the left nostril. After the count of five, close the left nostril, and hold the breath. Listen to your heartbeat and count till five. Keeping the left nostril closed, open the right nostril, and slowly breathe out to the count of 10. Feel the warm air in the right nostril. After the count of 10, breathe in slowly till the count of five. Feel the cool air in the right nostril. Now close the right nostril and hold the breath to the count of five. Count five beats of your heart. Open the left nostril and slowly breathe out to the count of 10. Feel the warm air in the

Figure 49. Anuloma viloma pranayama

left nostril. This makes one round. Practise five such rounds. Feeling the cool and warm air in the nostril and listening to the heartbeat will draw your attention from other things and increase watchfulness. After doing five rounds, open your eyes and feel the effect on your body and mind.

Bhastrika Pranayama

Breathe in with chest muscles forcefully, deeply and quickly and breathe out with chest muscles in the same way. This makes one round. You will sound like a bellow. Do not use the abdominal muscles. Practise 10 rounds. Stop and feel the tingling sensation on your face and fingertips. After three–four normal breaths, move to the next pranayama.

Bhramri Pranayama

Press the tragus of both ears with your thumbs to block the ear canals. Keep the index fingers on the eyebrows, middle fingers gently on the eyeballs, the ring fingers and the little fingers below the eyes. Keep the arms in line with shoulders. Close

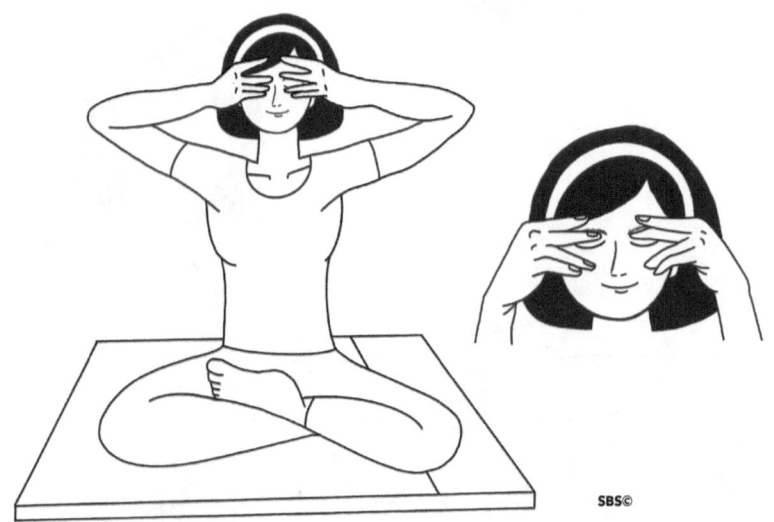

Figure 50. Bhramari pranayama

your lips and keep your teeth apart. Breathe in deeply. Now breathe out slowly through the nose while making the sound 'nnnnnnnnnnn' loudly to create vibrations in the oral cavity. Feel the vibrations in your palate and the head. Visualize the vibrations reaching the pineal and pituitary glands in the brain. This will activate both the glands. On finishing exhalation, take another deep breath for the second round. Practise three rounds, then bring your hands down. Open your eyes and feel the effect on the body and the mind.

Rapid Anuloma Viloma Pranayama

Sit in the same position as that of *Anuloma Viloma Pranayama*. The right elbow is kept touching the chest instead of keeping it at level of the shoulder. Inhale deeply from the left nostril and forcefully exhale from the right nostril. Now inhale deeply from the right nostril, and forcefully exhale from the left nostril. This is one round. Practise 10–15 rounds at a fast pace. Stop and bring the right hand down. Breathe normally and listen to the quickened heartbeat. Let the heartbeat settle, then do the next pranayama.

Figure 51. Rapid anuloma viloma pranayama

Udarshwasan Pranayama

Exhale forcefully by contracting the abdominal muscles and inhale deeply by expanding the abdominal muscles. Initially you may keep left palm on the abdomen to guide the abdominal muscles. Once learnt, it may not be required. Practise it for 10 rounds. Feel the effect on your body and mind.

Om, Aameen, Amen Chanting

Keep your eyes closed. Breathe in deeply through the nose. While breathing out slowly and steadily through the mouth, loudly create the sound ooohhhhmmmmmnnnnnn. Feel the resonance in the chest cavity for two-third part of the sound. Then close your lips and continue to breathe out through the nose while continuing the sound. Feel the vibrations through the nasal cavity. Do it three times. Keep your eyes closed and feel the effect of the vibrations on the body and mind. While keeping the eyes closed, practice visualization and gratitude before ending the session.

Visualization

Visualization means the formation of a mental image or a picture of something, not present before you. It is a creative ability. It projects a possibility in future. It is a part of will and intention. It is a universal rule that energy follows intention. Planting an image or thought in mind is like planting an electrode in the brain. Once it is planted, it takes hold and produces the desired effect. Practise visualization in the following sequence:

> Visualize a healthy glowing body. Feel a flame around your body. Draw your intention to the part of the body which you wish to heal. Feel it as healed.
>
> Visualize tranquillity and peace in thoughts. Feel it.

Visualize happiness in emotion. Feel that happiness and resolve to keep it the whole day.

Visualize harmony of your soul with other souls. Feel it and resolve to keep it the whole day. Pass on these vibrations of health, tranquillity, happiness and harmony to the person you wish to send.

Gratitude

Be grateful to yourself for working on your wellness, to the divine and the environment for blessing you with wellness. After some time, rub your palms together and put the cupped hands on your closed eyes. Feel the warmth and energy. Blink three times in the darkness of cupped hands. Open your eyes and remove the hands.

TIBETAN RITES

Ancient wisdom holds the key

Tibetan rites have been perfected by lamas in Tibetan monasteries. These are called rites because in Tibet every aspect of life relates to religion. There are seven rites. You can begin with one and try to stay at it consistently. As you gain strength, you can add more rites. Gradually, you will be able to practise all. Initially practice each rite three times a day for the first week. Then every week, increase the daily repetition by two till you reach 21 times a day.

Practise all rites in a set of 21 times per day for at least four months. Then you may do all of them in the evening if you are inclined. Go slow and gradually increase the second set of repetitions. You may skip a day in a week at the most.

Rest within the rites. Stand erect with your hands on the hips. Breathe deeply and rhythmically several times. As you breathe out, imagine the tension, disease and sickness leaving you. As you breathe in, imagine the body being filled with health, happiness and youthfulness.

Be aware of your body movements, breathing, final posture and its effect on the body. Feel the body returning to normal.

First Rite

It is a whirling rite. Stand erect with arms outstretched on the sides and parallel to the floor. Focus your vision on a single point straight ahead. Start whirling from left to right. As you begin to turn, continue to hold your vision on that point for as long as possible. Then turn your head around quickly and refocus on that point as soon as you can. This way you will become less dizzy. Initially, do it slowly three to four times, and stop if you feel even slightly dizzy. If not, then do up to six rounds in the first week. If you feel dizzy, sit or lie down. Gradually, increase the speed and number of rounds, but stop when you feel slightly dizzy. Do not go beyond 21 times as that will be more harmful than being helpful.

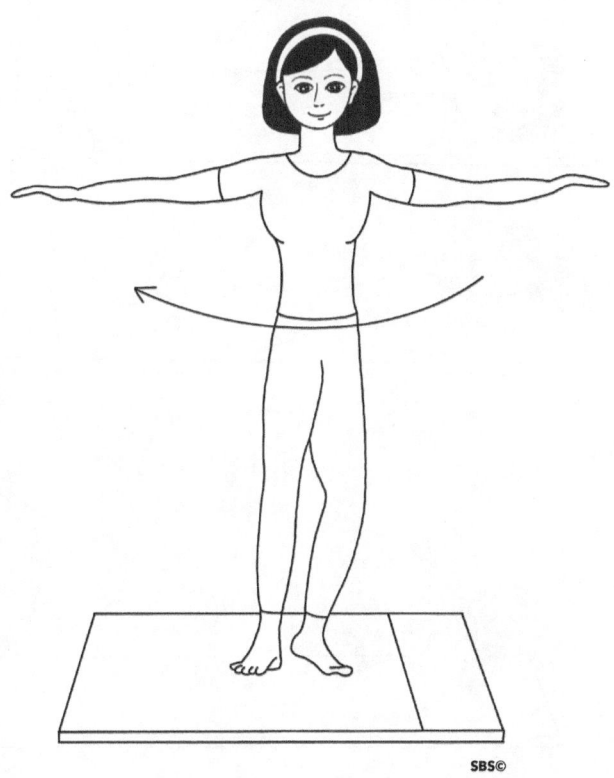

Figure 52. First rite

Second Rite

Lie down on your back on a mat. Keep your arms on the sides of the body with palms on the floor. Relax all muscles. Breathe in deeply and raise your head off the floor. Touch the chin to the chest. Simultaneously lift your legs together up in a vertical position. As far as possible do not bend the legs at the knees. It may be difficult initially, but it can be done with practice. Try to bring your legs closer to the head, but do not bend the knees. Hold the final position for a second or two. Breathe normally. Then breathe out and slowly lower the head and legs with knees kept straight to the floor. Relax all the muscles before repeating it. Continue breathing in and breathing out slowly and deeply while the muscles are relaxing. The deeper you breathe, the better you will feel.

Figure 53. Second rite

If you cannot keep the knees straight, then let them bend as necessary. Gradually, try to straighten them as much as possible. You can also start by lifting the legs in a bent position so that the knees are straight up and the feet are hanging down. Slowly make the legs straight.

Third Rite

Kneel on the floor with your body erect. Place your hands along the side of the thigh muscles. Bend the head forward to touch your chin to the chest. Inhale deeply, and slowly move the head and neck backwards as far as possible. Simultaneously lean backwards by arching the spine. Brace your arms and hands against the thighs for support. Hold for some time and continue to breathe deeply. Exhale completely and return to the original position. Relax for some time before repeating. You may keep your eyes closed for mental peace.

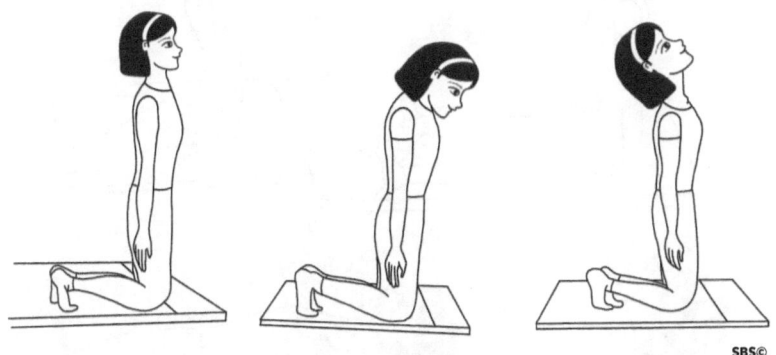

Figure 54. Third rite

Fourth Rite

Sit on the floor with legs straight out in front of you. Keep your feet about 12 inches apart. Keep the trunk of the body erect. Place the palms of your hands on the floor along the hips. Touch the chin to the chest. Breathe in deeply and drop the head backwards as far as it can go and simultaneously raise the hips and the body upwards so that the knees bend while the arms remain straight. The trunk of the body will be in a straight line with the upper legs. In the final position, the arms and lower legs will be straight and perpendicular to the floor and the body will be horizontal. At this point tense all the muscles in the body for a few seconds. Hold your breath as you tense your muscles. Now breathe out, relax all muscles and return to the original sitting position. Rest for some time and then repeat. Continue breathing deeply while resting. This rite gets perfected gradually in a month especially in older people. Do not get discouraged if you cannot do it in the first few attempts.

Figure 55. Fourth rite

Fifth Rite

Support the body with hands. Place your palms on the floor and toes in a flexed position. Keep hands and feet two feet apart. Keep arms and legs straight. Let your arms be perpendicular to the floor. The spine will be arched to put the body in a sagging position almost touching the floor. Breathe in and throw the head as far back as possible. Then raise the hips and bring the body up into an inverted 'V'. At the same time, touch the chin to the chest. Tense all the muscles of the body for a moment at the raised position. Hold your breath when the muscles are tense. Now breathe out, relax the muscles and return to the original position. At the final position of sagging, tense the muscles again for a moment. Hold the breath. Breathe in and start again.

Sixth Rite

Figure 56. Fifth rite

Sixth Rite

This rite is more suitable for men because in women the natural voice is shrill and making it baritone will be unnatural. Slowly breathe in and fill your lungs. Now breathe out slowly while creating the prolonged sound 'om' in as low a tone as possible. Divide it roughly half and half between 'oooohhhhhhhh' and 'mmmmmmnnnnn'. Feel the 'oohhhhh' vibrate through the chest cavity and 'mmmmmmnnnnn' through nasal cavities. The vibration of sound is significant, not the act of making the sound or the meaning of sound. Go on repeating while lowering your voice more and more in steps until you have forced it as low as possible. Practise in the morning when the voice quality tends to be in the lower pitch. Practise this exercise in the bathroom and hear your voice reverberate.

During the day consciously lower the pitch of your voice. Listen to yourself while you speak. If you hear yourself becoming higher or shrill, adjust your voice to a lower pitch. Keep your voice in the lower pitch as much as possible throughout the day. Lowering the pitch of the vocal cords increases the vibrations felt at the fifth chakra located at the base of the neck. This normalises its spinning. All the chakras are connected to each other, but the fifth chakra is more connected to the first chakra, which regulates the body's sexual centre. Once these two speed up, all the seven chakras will vibrate at normal speed.

Seventh Rite

This rite is for becoming a superhuman. Attempt it after you have practised other rites for two years or have gained your sexual energy and have decided to become a celibate. This will make you look dramatically younger, but you must decide if you can become a celibate. Perform it when you feel excess sexual energy and there is a natural desire for its expression. Do not suppress that desire. Instead, transmute it with the help of this rite.

Stand erect. Slowly exhale all the air out of your lungs. Simultaneously bend over and put your hands on the knees. Now force the last trace of air out. Then with empty lungs, return to a straight position. Place your hands on your hips and press on them. This will push your shoulders up. Simultaneously pull the abdomen in as much as possible, and raise the chin. Hold this position for as long as you can. When you are finally forced to take air into your empty lungs, let the air flow in through your nose to fill the lungs. Then exhale through the mouth. As you exhale, relax your arms, letting them hang naturally at your sides. Inhale deeply through your nose, and exhale completely several times through the mouth. This is one round. Three repetitions are the maximum required to redirect sexual energy to the seven vortices.

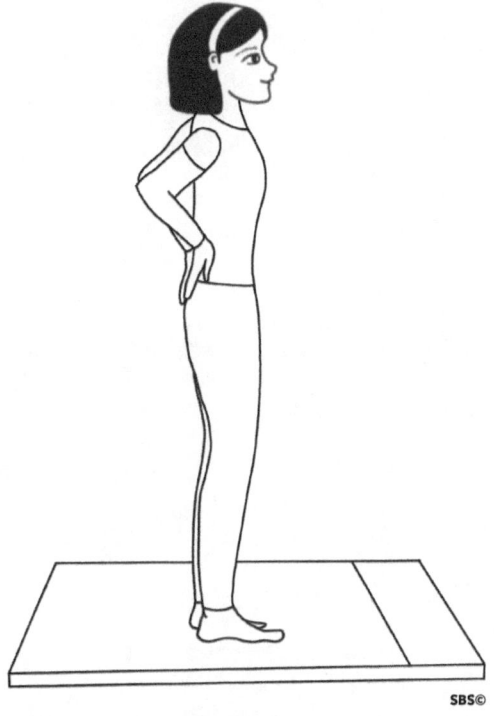

Figure 57. Seventh rite

Attempt it only if you have active sexual urge. Else, there is nothing to transmute, and the rite will be a futile exercise. Do it only if you are genuinely motivated. If you feel incomplete in terms of sexual expression and must struggle to overcome its expression, then this may not be right for you, because this rite will be a struggle and will cause inner conflict leading to unwellness.

These rites can be done by themselves or combined with wellness exercises. Either way, follow them with pranayama, visualization and gratitude.

WAY TO MENTAL WELLNESS

See the mind to silence it

The way to mental wellness is subtle, covert and complex as compared to physical wellness, which is gross, overt and simple. It will be worth reading the chapter on mental wellness again to grasp the present chapter better. The preventive aspect of mental wellness is through attitude management. The curative aspect is through measures for immediate relief, prolonged relief and permanent relief.

Attitude Management

The state of mental wellness is directly influenced by one's attitude at any given point of time. In fact, what posture is to physical wellness, attitude is to mental wellness. Attitude management is the starting point.

Attitude is the way you look at the world. It is a settled way of thinking or perceiving a situation or person. Your attitude is the outcome of your memory which gives you a mental conditioning, which becomes a default setting. It dictates how you respond to situations. It is not easy to change the setting, but developing a positive attitude is possible. This may be done in the following ways:

Reprogramme yourself

A stressful life is likely to make your mind agitated. The wellness way of life will create an inward calm so that everyday living does not cause distress, at least for long periods. This will reprogramme you to project peace, love and harmony, instead of violence, hate and conflict.

Change your Outlook

You cannot change the world, but you can change the way you look at the world. This way you hit the nail on the head. The world can no longer give you any distress.

> *'Aankh mein parakh ho to dekh,*
> *Husan se pur hai kul jahaan;*
> *Bande ki nazar ka hai kusur,*
> *Jalwon ki kuchh kami nahin.'*

'If you are discerning, then the world is full of beauty. It is the eye of the beholder that is at fault, as there is no dearth of grandeur in the world.' Your outlook is not a switch that can be turned on or off. You must develop and maintain it.

Never Feel Hopeless

Hope means you are not giving up. Hope creates a ray of light even in the darkest hours of life for a better tomorrow, because of which life

goes on actively. The absence of hope is a state of neutrality. Life may still go on, but in a dull and inactive way. Hopelessness is negative and damaging because you have given up on life. You have been defeated. Hopelessness will make you unwell.

Lord Krishna had a very difficult life, but always maintained his equipoise. Krishna's son, Pradyuman, died when his Yadava clan fought amongst themselves. For the first time, Krishna felt hopeless and retreated to the jungle. In the jungle, a tribal mistook his black foot to be an animal and shot a poisonous arrow that killed Krishna. Existence removed godly Krishna when he succumbed to human frailties.

Start every day with hope, and finish it in contentment. Be satisfied with whatsoever you have achieved that day. There will be another day, another life, God willing! This understanding is the seed of hope.

Maintain your willpower. When the going gets tough, the tough get going!

> *'Yeh na kabhi samajhana mushkil hai zindagi,*
> *Himmat ki sirf baat hai chaman hai zindagi.'*

'Never ever take life as a difficulty. If you maintain your willpower, then life is like a garden in bloom.' Keep this couplet in mind when you encounter impediments, setbacks, despair and despondency in your life.

Accept yourself

Most people do not accept themselves. Inability to accept the way they are causes too much unrest in their lives. Accept your body, mind, intellect and potential. Accept your anger, your desires and drives too. Do not suppress. Do not feel guilty. Do not fight with desires. Let them come. Face them with readiness; else, from the murky depths of the subconscious, they will trouble you.

Accept your deficiencies. Do not demean yourself. It is okay to be dissatisfied, as that will be a driving force to improve yourself to the extent feasible, but laugh it off, if you cannot. Do not ruin your self-worth.

Grow old gracefully. The more you try to hide your age, the more you are phoney. Relax and let time run its natural course. It will give you peace in return.

Accept Others

Once you have accepted yourself only then you will be able

to accept others because you will see in them all that is also in you. This humbles you. Evaluate but do not judge others. Understand that others are acting from their perspective, which may differ from yours. View their actions dispassionately. Encourage their potential because potential improves when circumstances change. With this understanding, it will be easier for you to accommodate and accept them. Once you accept others, they may accept you.

Watch your Response

The mind creates conflict if the new inputs, by any situation, contradict the old information held in the mind. How you deal with conflict is in your hands. If the watcher in you is strong, then the conflict cannot overpower you and cause reactionary response.

One always wishes to associate with what one likes, but sometimes the situation becomes contrary. You come across inimical people whom you do not like. Do not get perturbed. They are teachers who test whether you have been successful in dropping your conditioning.

Analyse your Behaviour

Be mindful of how you behave in a stressful situation. For instance, how do you respond to failure? Observe your own feelings. Do they make you feel scared, vulnerable and lonely? Or do you approach failure as a moment of reflecting on an error of judgement that you could not possibly foresee? It is important to bear in mind that your role is to respond, not react. Reactionary behaviour will only worsen the state of your mental health.

Be Natural

Being natural is never stressful. We feel stressed when we are not our truest selves. Do not try to impress anyone. Do not unnecessarily suppress your true feelings. Express them, if possible, but gently. Impressing and suppressing cause tension. Do not copy anyone. You will lose your originality.

Avoid Expectation

Expectation is precursor to frustration. Do not set out on this journey, so expect nothing from others, yourself and even God. You will never feel frustrated. Take the results of each action as a bonus. This saves you from disappointment if things do not work out the way you had thought.

Be Self-sufficient

Try to reduce your need to find happiness in things which are not in your control. You are alive, and that is sufficient cause for joy. Follow your attractions, but if you do not get what you wanted, then accept the situation rather than reacting to it.

Avoid Comparing your Life

Every creation is unique. It is futile to compare two people when each is distinct in his own way. Comparison will either make you inferior or superior, and both cause mental turmoil. Comparison causes unnecessary frustration because you cannot change the way you are. Likewise, it is not always possible to have in your life what others have.

Creativity Keeps you Positive

Dreams become smaller when we advance in age. Dream big. Dr A. P. J. Abdul Kalam used to say, 'Dreaming small is a crime.' Return to the society your experiences of life. This is creativity in old age. You have wasted your old age if you are not creative.

Always be Young in Thoughts

Keep your inner child alive. Maintain childlike innocence.

Innocence means no preconceived ideology. Every moment is new. Nurture this no matter how old you grow.

Amrita Pritam gave a new perspective to youthfulness in her autobiography, *Rasidi Ticket*. She said, 'If atrocities are being committed anywhere in the world and you raise your voice against them, then you are only sixteen years of age irrespective of how old you are.' This spirit of youthfulness keeps you mentally fit.

Despite all the efforts on attitude management, the mind still sneaks in. Some interim measures are suggested to help the mind get rid of stressful situations.

Immediate Relief Measures

Relaxation restores all the systems and revitalizes all the cells of the body. It is easy to look at the source of stress when you are relaxed. You can confront the cause, and see it in a new light. You can watch your habituated reactions and choose to remain undisturbed. Auto suggestion and visualization is possible. Try the following measures to relax when you are acutely distressed:

Watch your Breath and Listen to your Heartbeat

This will divert your mind from emotionally charged thoughts. You will stop brooding. The body will be at ease and the mind will be at peace. In a few minutes you will feel relaxed.

Indulge in Repetitive Behaviour

Repetitive behaviour like pacing back and forth or tapping your pen on the desk stimulates secretion of serotonin, which reduces anxiety.

Make your Body Still

Become immobile. Relax your muscles. Observe how it feels. This stops the signals from your muscles to your brain and vice versa. It will make you feel relaxed.

Take Control of the Situation

Gaining control, even if it is very small, produces DHEA[1], which enhances wellness in many ways.

Prolonged Relief Measures

Engage in Pleasurable Physical Activity

Play with your pet or go for a run rather than watching a screen or playing video games. This helps release dopamine, which makes you happy. Running increases the supply of oxygen and glucose to the brain. It also releases endorphin, which gives a sense of well-being. It also increases BDNF[2] for the production of new cells.

Laughter Therapy

Charlie Chaplin once famously said, 'A day without laughter is a day wasted.' Laughter is the best medicine. Laughing is a natural tonic, which gives peace of mind, enhances respiratory capacity and increases blood circulation in the body. At Jindal Naturecure Institute, Bengaluru, laughter therapy is part of the natural therapies. Laughing naturally or even unnaturally for 10 minutes every day works wonders for the body and mind.

Practise Death Posture

Lie down and become immobile like a dead body. Visualize that your soul has come out of your body and is watching you from above. Feel the relaxation of being dead. Try to hold this visualization for long and stay in the moment.

---

[1] Dehydroepiandrosterone is a hormone produced in the adrenal gland, which helps produce testosterone and estrogen.

[2] Brain derived neurotrophic factor

Tense and Relax the Whole Body Alternately

Lie down on your back on the mat. Support your head with a small pillow. Keep the arms on the floor beside your body. Keep the palms open and facing the floor. Breathe in deeply. Hold the breath inside and raise the legs, shoulders and arms off the ground, but not more than 15 centimetres. Keep your arms and legs straight and point the palms towards the feet. Keep feet stretched outwards. Stretch and tense the whole body. Feel that every muscle is tense. Maintain this position to a slow count of 10 or whatever is comfortable. Do not overstrain. Then breathe out deeply, relax the muscles and bring the body back to the floor. Stay this way for one minute or till the count of 60. Perform it three times. If initially you cannot lift the arms and legs, simply tense the whole body while remaining on the ground. But try to raise the body gradually. Feel the relaxation in your body and mind. You can repeat it one more time and then proceed to the next stage of relaxation.

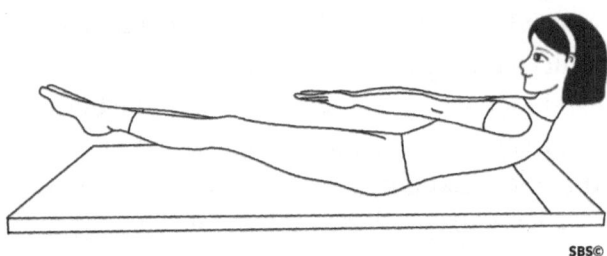

Figure. 58. Pose for making the whole body tense.

Relax as in Deep Sleep but without Sleeping

After the above exercise, keep lying down on your back. Keep your arms on the sides of the body, but a little away so that they do not touch the body. Keep the palms open and upwards. Do not clench the fingers. Keep the legs straight and slightly apart. Close your eyes. Feel the hips on the floor. Release if there is any tension in the hip muscles. Feel the contact of heels with the floor. Feel that both your legs are limp. Feel the right and left arms in the same way. Release if there is any tension in the hands. Feel the shoulders touching the floor and relax them. Drop the lower jaw but keep the lips together, not pressed. The teeth should be slightly separated. Relax the face and any frown on the forehead. Feel the head heavy and limp on the floor. Feel the whole body so heavy that you cannot raise it. Watch the blankness with closed eyes. Feel the body floating in that blankness. Do not move the body at all. Be thoughtless. Stay in this position for as long as possible. After some time, become aware of the natural rhythm of your breath. Do not change it. Be aware of the breath going in and then coming out. Feel all anxiety and tension leave your body with the breath going out. Be alert so that you do not sleep. Stay awake to appreciate the deep relaxation. If you sleep, the mind will come back with its worries and problems. Follow the above steps systematically. Images of different parts of the body are stored in different areas of the brain. When you relax any part of the body, the corresponding part of the brain also relaxes.

Mental Dusting

Silence and Solitude

Select a period every day or once in a week during which you neither speak nor think or meet anyone. This silence and solitude will make you aware of the constant chattering of your mind and your feelings. If you miss anything during this period, it will show that you are feeling lonely. Loneliness is misery. Drop the cause of your loneliness. Feel your aloneness. You are your only companion. To be alone is blissful. You will become so silent that others too will become silent in your presence.

Watch your Mind

Find the source of your aversions, resentments, attachments, unhappiness, anger and desires. Once you have known the source, observe your attitude that has caused these feelings. Wilfully release the cause and also your attitude. Watch these leaving you. It will clean the mind. Identify the factors which could be triggering stress in your life. Work your way out by addressing them one at a time.

Diary Writing

Writing can be cathartic. Instead of denying or suppressing your emotions, it is better to write them in a diary. It will maintain your privacy. When I[3] was sick, I maintained a detailed diary of my thoughts and emotions. Every time I wrote, I felt lighter and better. However, I never read what I had written, because I was too afraid that reading it would feed my mind with what I had just eliminated and the vicious circle would go on. Having recovered, I simply discarded those diaries.

Maintain Social Contacts

Be in the company of friends, spiritually inclined persons and spiritual teachers. This reduces mental tension and opens the door to tranquillity. Stay in touch with a person you admire and trust. Human touch releases oxytocin that makes you calm. This is how hugging works.

Examine your Thoughts and Feelings before you Sleep

You can view the pros and cons of your activities. Drop what pushes you towards unwellness. Continue the ones that bring you into wellness.

---

[3] S. B. Sehajpal

Mind Fasting

Toxins build up in the mind too. All unpleasant experiences will become toxic and cause pathological changes if they are not cleaned out. Thus, it is important to detoxify the mind.

Physically Remove yourself from Stressful Environment

The change of scene is akin to change of food during fasting. Visit places that give you peace and happiness. During my days of distress, I6 visited many religious places. This calmed me down. I felt the grip of stress loosening. I observed the plight of many other visitors who had come there to find solutions to their problems. I wondered whether they were suffering because of others or themselves. It dawned on me that, in my case, I had created my suffering through my reactions. I could also understand that these reactions must stop, and the only person who can stop these is me. This proved to be a turning point for me.

Nature Creates Positive Impressions
The artificial world gives junk impressions and negativity. Step outdoors and spend some time in the lap of nature. It will also limit your exposure to persons or situations that involve criticism, judgement or ridicule, and, thus, reduce the flow of negative energy. William Henry Davies has aptly said:

> 'What is this life so full of care,
> We have no time to stand and stare.'

All the above solutions subdue the mind but only for some time. The mind gets fully absorbed in any activity or sleep, but as the activity ceases or one wakes up, the mind returns to its original state because of its default setting. What is the way out?

Permanent Relief Measure

Meditation

Meditation is a state of consciousness in which the mind surrenders its power of control and allows the soul to guide the body-mind. The surrender of mind means that no thought or emotion is generated by the mind during that time. There are no contents for your mind to dwell on—the mind ceases to be, or we may say, it is a state of 'no mind'.

Meditation is silence. Science cannot detect silence. Hence, meditation cannot be a scientific study. It can only be a personal revelation. Meditation is repose. The soul hibernates without repose. Repossess your soul by being in a state of unoccupied, empty and silent mind, with no idea of doing anything, neither going nor rushing anywhere.

How meditation calms the mind?

Your soul is deathless. Meditation makes you understand your deathlessness. This brings in immense maturity, and the child in you, who was happy playing to the tunes of the body and mind, grows up. Meditation takes you to a realm which is beyond your work, head and heart centres. It is a passage from mental wellness to spiritual wellness.

Meditation means to be in the present, free from the past and future, just being here and now. Time disappears when you meditate. That is why you feel joy. You experience a sense of eternity. In meditation, the ego disappears, and with that the idea of your separation from existence also disappears. This ushers in tremendous harmony.

Meditation makes the mind visible. When the mind is under observation, it is not restless. In fact, it obeys the soul, its master, to offload its contents. Meditation also makes you aware of what unsettles you. This realisation itself is enough to drop such activities.

Normally you remain confined to your intellectual mind. But meditation allows you to go beyond the intellectual mind and connect with the collective mind. This makes you aware of your ancestral past and the near future. This is the invisible reality which affects you all the time.

Meditation opens the deeper layers of mind where fears, hatred, dislike, jealousy, inferiority complexes and all other negativity is stored. These are the invisible mental afflictions doing all the mischief. Your soul watches these, and in the process, they show up and burst like a bubble when it reaches the surface. These releases happen even if the conditions that caused these accumulations are not sorted out. That is why meditation is also called 'samadhi'. A *'samadhan'* (resolution) has happened and erased the problem. This activity happens when you are awake and not under the effect of any drugs or alcohol, etc., and that is why the solution is permanent.

How meditation helps wellness?

Freedom from an unsettled mind is the only freedom. When the mind is quiet, it ceases to disturb your equilibrium. You feel at peace because your thoughts and emotions, which are the products of mind, become lesser. Gradually, the mind's grip over you loosens and you become more peaceful. During these periods of peace, you are in a space of bliss because the mind does not trouble you.

The world goes on at its pace, but you are unaffected with whatever is happening. The more you are in this space, the less the world bothers you.

How to meditate?

Become still in your body and silent in the mind, so that the soul can become evident to you. Be relaxed throughout the meditation period. Be playful. Do not become serious and tense.

Give yourself enough time, so that you do not rush your way through the happening of meditation. Do not have expectations and goals while meditating. On some days, it is easier to meditate and experience an inner peace and stillness while on other days, it does not happen at all. Do not get frustrated. Meditation is a knack. It comes on its own. You can only prepare the ground for it every day.

Create a sacred space

A tranquil environment builds up meditation the minute you enter it. Earmark a quiet space in your house where very few people enter. Use the same place every day. Go into this place at the same time every day. Wear the same dress. Use the same mat to sit. Light up the same essence to maintain the same aroma. If you are using sound to create a soothing atmosphere and drown any noises, then play the same music during the period of meditation. Every time you enter this space and meditate, you will leave behind your vibrations, which will be absorbed by you when you enter again. These vibrations get diluted and polluted if frequent visitors who do not meditate, enter this space. This is how the space for meditation becomes sacred. Sit in this space any time you feel oppressed. The vibrations will lift you up.

Sit in chin mudra as explained in watchfulness. Keep the spine erect so that you stay alert and do not doze off.

Increase watchfulness

Slowly and deeply fill your lungs with air as per your comfort level. Now slowly breathe out through the mouth while chanting the sound 'om/aameen/amen' through the chest cavity. Feel the vibrations in the chest cavity. Feel how the vibrations are travelling to the abdomen and all other body parts. After some time, close the lips and continue to breathe out through your nostrils so that the 'nnnnnnnnnn' sound resonates through the nasal cavity. Feel the vibrations in your nose, on the face, head, eyes and ears.

The lower the tone of chanting, the more effective will be the vibrations, because then you will have to be very attentive to listen to the sound and feel its effect. Practise audible chanting three times. Now chant silently without making any sound. Feel the vibrations in your chest cavity and then in the nasal cavity. Your watchfulness will become sharper. Repeat it thrice. Stop chanting. Feel the absence of sound vibrations. This will make your watchfulness very intense.

Watch your thoughts

Watch them to see what they are up to. Become aware of the space between the observer and thoughts. This space will allow your watchfulness to divide itself between the mind and soul. This division initiates communication. The monologue of the mind becomes a dialogue with the soul. A solution is possible in a dialogue. A dialogue is a catharsis and adds to wellness. A monologue is a burden that causes unwellness. A dialogue with oneself is self-counselling.

Look for the source of the thought. How did the thought come about? Continue the search by travelling backwards till you can go no further. Pass no judgement during this examination. Feel no identification with anything. The constant stream of thoughts shall slow down on its own. Look for the gap between the two thoughts. This is the space where the mind ceases. Identify and stay in this gap. A thought has gone, then a gap occurs, before another thought comes. Initially, it will only be a moment, but as you progress in practice it will go on increasing to a point where it is up to you to allow a thought or keep the gap vacant of thought. It is now that you are the master of your mind.

Watch your emotions

What is it that you are feeling? What is this feeling doing to you? How is it affecting your wellness? Why do you feel the way you do? What is the source? Let all hidden emotions connected with that source come up. Examine them and wilfully release them in space and feel the weight lifting. Feel this lightness. Deep-seated habits and memories float to the surface so that we can let them go and become free from them.

Now bring your awareness to the *sahasrara chakra* on top of the head. Initially, you may not feel anything, but with gradual practice, this chakra will start responding. You will feel a tingling sensation which will become prominent as a circular movement in a clockwise direction. Stay there for a minute or so and feel connected to the universe.

Now bring your awareness to the *agya chakra* between the two eyebrows. You will start feeling a tingling sensation in a clockwise movement. Stay there. Through this chakra, connect with the divine. Make a request and feel the wish being granted. Express your gratitude for that.

Observe the vacant space

Freedom from thoughts and emotions prepares you for observation of the vacant space. This is the final stage of meditation. In this stage, the observer is present, but there is nothing to observe, neither of the body nor of the mind. The field of vision has no content. There is only space without content. The soul is observing itself. There is infinite space without boundaries. It is infinity. There is a void in which there are no opposites, hence no judgements. There is no right or wrong, no darkness or light, no ifs and buts, no negative and positive. Awareness observes itself. Buddha has spoken of space beyond this. He has called it '*shunya*', meaning nothingness. This state, according to Buddha, signifies the absence of even your soul. Stay in it for as long as it stays.

Usually, it is not more than a minute or so. If you can stay for 40 minutes, then you are a yogi. This state takes you to the realm of collective super consciousness (illuminating mind) and cosmic consciousness (intuitive mind). This is the state of bliss. When this state is reached even for a few moments, it helps you attain complete mental and spiritual wellness. If you do not reach the state of bliss, you still experience mental peace and remain in a state of mental balance.

Chant om thrice

Terminate your session by chanting Om thrice in low tone. Rub your hands vigorously, and place the cupped hands on your eyes. Blink in the darkness three times and open your eyes. Remove the hands and view the surroundings. You will feel a change in your surroundings from the point when you started the meditation. Though the surroundings are the same, your acuity of observation has improved.

How to evaluate your meditation?

Meditation is passive. It does not need energy. If you are tired after meditation, be assured you have not meditated. Post meditation, your emotional outbursts will decrease. You will not grab, deceive and cheat. You will become very sensitive to all that is around, but it will not disturb your silence. Guru Nanak Dev ji said, 'One who does not derive pleasure out of comfort and does not feel suffering in discomfort, is a true human.' If you maintain equanimity in either situation, then you are in meditation all the time.

WAY TO SPIRITUAL WELLNESS

Let the soul shine through your body and mind

Spiritual wellness is the most delicate and difficult because it is abstract, mysterious and requires that each person must lay one's own track. The other person's path is only an indication, a finger pointing to the moon, but undertaking the journey to it is your individual effort.

Love is to spiritual wellness what posture is to physical wellness or attitude is to mental wellness. Unless you have loved in your life, you cannot attain spiritual wellness. This statement is difficult to digest because, lust masquerades as love, due to which our understanding of love itself is wrong. Lust keeps you attached to the body and mind. Love takes you beyond both. Lust enslaves, love liberates. If you have not perceived love in your heart, then you cannot perceive your soul because both are abstract.

Unless you love yourself, you cannot undertake self-actualization. Self-realization comes after self-actualization. You make the passive soul active, which means you have given birth to your soul. Unless you love your soul, you cannot bear the hardships of its birth and nurturing. Unless the mother loves the child, she cannot bear the pain of childbirth and hardships of rearing the child.

There are three main approaches to spiritual wellness: *bhakti yog*, *gyan yog* and *karma yog*.

Bhakti Yog

Love is called '*preeti*' in Hindi. *Preeti* has four aspects. *Preeti* for youngsters is '*sneh*', for equals is '*prem*', for elders is '*shraddha*' and preeti for the divine is bhakti. If you do not have *sneh*, *prem* and *shraddha*, you cannot have bhakti in your heart. Devotion cannot arise till the lover sees the divine in their beloved.

Devotion is developed through prayerfulness—by singing and chanting in the praise of God, known as '*kirtan*' and recital of mantras known as '*japa*'. Devotion demands trust, which means directing unconditional love to the divinity and His creation. You trust the divine to see you through the pulls and pressures of life. Your ego, which tells you that you can solve the problems of life, vanishes. The devotee takes shelter (also known as '*sharan*' in Hindi) in God; hence, this approach is called '*sharnam*'.

Till the devotee has not merged into the divine, bhakti has not happened. Your body and mind cease to be in such a state. The soul becomes apparent to you. When you do not lose your faith despite the ups and downs of life, the divine bestows silence on you, which gives you spiritual wellness.

Gyan Yog

'*Vigyan*' means learning about things outside you while '*gyan*' means knowing your innermost. You get this knowledge through '*sravana*', meaning listening to sacred knowledge on spirituality; '*manana*', meaning reflecting and contemplating on the lessons learnt and finally '*nididhyasana*', which means meditation to practically see what you have gathered theoretically. This gyan will make your soul apparent to you.

You will see the soul and God in every aspect of His creation. The melody of love will engulf you. When you do not let your revelation get clouded, irrespective of the situations of life, only then you have reached spiritual wellness.

Karma Yog

Every action elicits a reaction. Action and reaction together make karma. If the reaction does not unfold at the time of action, then it gets accumulated. Accumulated reactions of our actions from millions of years of our existence are called '*sanchit karma*', where the term '*sanchit*' means accumulated. *Sanchit karma* lying in your store cannot be exhausted in one life, so only a small portion of it is given to everyone in one lifetime. Only this portion of karma becomes operative in that lifetime, the rest remains dormant. This small portion of karma is '*prarabdh*', meaning 'destiny'. You must exhaust your destiny of the present life by living it out. There is no other way. Edward Fitzgerald elucidates this in the following lines:

> '*The moving finger writes and having writ,*
> *Moves on; nor all your Piety nor Wit,*
> *Shall lure it back to cancel half a line,*
> *Nor all thy tears wash out a word of it.*'

This thought resonates with what Sant Kabir has said, 'The momentum of life destined for you cannot be changed.' Nemesis catches up with you.

According to the ancient Indian scripture *Padma Purana*, five aspects of your life are preordained. Birth, death, knowledge, wealth and fame are pre-decided by the cosmic mind because of various *karmic* inputs about you. What is preordained cannot be changed. Your destiny is part of the preordained. However, it is different for each one of us. That is why the sorrows and sufferings, the joys and happiness vary for each one of us, despite living under the same circumstances, in the same period and in the same environment.

While living out your destiny, you will create more karma. These new actions are called 'agami karma', where 'agami' means next. *Agami karmas* will get added to *sanchit karma*. This is how the cycle of *karma* goes on. What is the way out of the *karmic* cycle then? The answers lies in your free will.

Free Will

Humans are the only creatures with free will to choose how to live out their destiny. In this freedom to choose lies the secret of ending the *karmic* cycle.

You have freedom to accept or reject your destiny. Acceptance will give you tranquillity while rejection will cause turmoil. Accept your destiny because it is your own creation, your karma, and being unhappy with it will not change anything. Instead, it will make you more miserable.

When I[1] joined dental surgery, I was a bit unhappy as I was looking for medical profession. It was my mother who cleared the perspective by sharing these words of wisdom from Abdul Rahim Khan-I-Khana: 'In pursuit of bigger things of life, do not ignore the smaller ones, because where a needle is required the knife is of no use.'

Dental surgery was preordained for me, and I rose to the pinnacle of this profession in the Armed Forces— a destiny which no one could fathom when I joined it. We will reach where ever we are destined to. Your role is to go along happily with whatever is in store for you.

Your Reaction while Living Out your Destiny is also your Choice

You are free to either feel miserable, happy or stay in a state of equipoise while living out your destiny. It will affect your

---
[1] S. B. Sehajpal

wellness accordingly.

Your Effort is your Choice

Since you cannot know what is preordained and destined, the only thing you can do is to put in the utmost efforts, to make the best out of your circumstances. Do so without creating tension, stress and worrying for the fruit of labour, as that will be detrimental to wellness.

Act with Humility

It means to be aware that you are only an instrument, a medium through which an action is unfolding or being done, but you are not the doer. You become a spectator to the action happening, just a witness. You have no motive behind that action. It is an action performed without any expectation of reward. This is called *'nishkam karma'*. It is desireless, detached and selfless action. You do not allow your ego or sense of entitlement to take precedence or come in the way of your action. You act freely without worrying about the consequences. *Nishkam karma* does not create *agami karma*. When you are not looking for rewards, it is easier for you to accept whatever is the result. There will be no unrest. This is spiritual wellness. Unless you love what you do, you cannot perform *nishkam karma*.

If in one lifetime you have gladly accepted your destiny and put in your best efforts without getting attached to the consequence of the action, then all the *sanchit karma* till that birth will be destroyed. The cycle of *karma* will end forever.

Lord Mahavira was a *karma yogi*. He advocated that the state in which you are living is only your creation. Tackle the situations yourself till you resolve them. This approach is called *'shraman'*, where *'shram'* means effort.

Charvaka and Epicurian Approach

Rishi Charvaka in the eastern world and Epicurus in the western world have expounded a different thought for spiritual wellness. They advocated eating, drinking and being merry despite the situations in life. Enjoy the pleasures of life. Dance away your blues. Do not complain about anything. You can do this only if you love yourself and everybody else. This way of life also gives you silence. Live in that silence, and you will attain spiritual wellness.

Religious Ceremonies

Do religious ceremonies add to wellness? The answer is both yes and no.

Yes, because these rituals remove you, at least for some time, from the environment in which you are inclined to commit mischief and indulge in actions that are the very cause of your unwellness. During religious activities, you are free from negativity. Your vibrations become positive. Whether you ask for these positive vibes or not, you receive them by simply being in that religious group. In religious ceremonies you draw inspiration and assurance from other group members. You might have stopped if you were alone. God is the primordial silence, which can be communicated only through silence. Your verbal prayer is only sound, but you must do it till you become capable of singing through silence.

No, because all ceremonies are external. They do not change you much on the inside. You carry out religious ceremonies with the expectation of a reward. It is merely a negotiation. But God is not a businessman!

Acceptance and Surrender

All paths of spiritual wellness take you to a point where you accept everything, even the inimical. Acceptance leads to peaceful coexistence. The test of acceptance is gratitude. It means that you are able to internalize the following feeling: I have no complaints, desires or demands. You accept the will of God. In acceptance slight trace of doing is still there. However, surrender is a step ahead. When doing stops, being happens. Being is surrender. Surrender is submission, an inner gentleness and silence so that no questioning arises. Surrender to a person is slavery. Surrender to a presence is liberation. God is that presence.

Surrender is a passive, feminine approach. Acceptance is an active, masculine approach. Lust is masculine. Love is feminine. Without love, the feminine cannot perform the role of mother assigned to it. Mystics suggest that ultimately men are born as women, from where they get liberated. The masculine has always suppressed the feminine. For centuries men have ruled the world and denied women their due place. In the present century, women are making their mark in every field. Is evolution trying to make the world peaceful through women?

Freedom in Present Life

We become free from life when we die, but a person who has reached self-realization becomes free from life while being alive. Such a person is free from the sufferings of life. He passes through this world unaffected. The famous Urdu poet Akbar Allahabadi has summed up this sentiment in the following lines:

> 'Duniya mein hoon duniya ka talabgar nahin hoon,
> Bazar se guzra hoon khareedar nahin hoon.'

'I live in the world, but I have no desires of the world. I am passing through this marketplace, but I am not a buyer.'

Freedom in the Next Life

A person who has experienced freedom in the present life

passes away from this world knowingly and peacefully. Such a person takes the next birth, if he so desires, and that too with a destiny of his choice. This is 'nirvana', which means liberation.

Allama Iqbal has written:

'Khudi ko kar buland itna, ki har taqdeer se pehle,
Khuda bande se khud poochhe, bata teri raza kya hai?'

'Achieve such lofty heights in your life, that God himself will ask, what do you want to do now?' If such a person opts out of rebirth, he gets 'moksha', meaning 'release' from the cycle of birth and death. Then there is no returning to this world.

WAY TO BLISSFULNESS

Bliss is the birthright

One experiences bliss for the first time in the womb, when one was sitting silently and doing nothing. However, it changes with birth. You must breathe now. Your mother cannot do it for you. The doing has started and will never end. Bliss in the womb makes you long for blissfulness. So you go on searching it for the rest of your life. When you seek pleasure through the senses of your body, you are actually looking for that bliss. You will not get it because this approach itself is wrong. Bliss is beyond sensual pleasures.

Bliss is your nature. It will come when you stop seeking. Blissfulness happens on its own. It happens when the wellness of all other layers has been achieved. One cannot jump to blissfulness without taking care of other aspects of wellness.

Bliss is not your achievement, because in the state of blissfulness there is nobody in you who can say that I have achieved bliss. If it is so that means you still have ego. The 'I' gets subsumed in the soul before blissfulness happens. The space created by the absence of your ego gets filled up with blissfulness.

All the wellness practices are aimed at yourself. Go beyond

yourself. Reach out to others in need, without any expectation in return. This may help add to your blissfulness.

In a state of bliss, time ceases for you. You do not travel to the past and the future. You live only in the present. If you live in the moment, blissfulness will come to you automatically as a gift from the beyond.

WAY TO GODLINESS AND GOD

Existence flows through emptiness

Godliness descends on you. It is a blessing showered on you by God. It is given and cannot be claimed. If you have the desire for it and you try to achieve it with a design, then you will never get it. All your efforts and hard work only prepare the ground to make you empty. God will not descend till you are not empty. It may take aeons to prepare grounds, but grace can descend in a jiffy. Some instances are being shared below to understand how little time it takes for the descent of His grace.

Prophet Mohammad, peace be upon Him, was in his bed when he was called by the divine for grace. When he returned, the bed was still warm and the water from the cup, which his foot had spilled while getting up, was still pouring out.

When Jesus was being crucified, he called out to God saying, 'Oh father! Why have you forsaken me?' He realized his mistake that he was complaining and not accepting the cross as the will of God. Jesus immediately corrected to say, 'Thy Will be done.' In that moment, God's grace descended upon him; from Jesus, he became Christ.

Gautama tried to find God for nearly 12 years. One day, he decided to drop all efforts. That evening he slept very soundly because there was no desire to try anymore. On waking up, he saw the morning star fading away. In that moment, he decided to also let Gautama fade away. In doing that, Gautama became Buddha.

Guru Nanak Dev ji, while counting bags of grain at the granary he worked, uttered the number 'thirteen'. Thirteen is pronounced as *'tera'* in Punjabi language, but it also means 'yours'. One word and the enlightenment dawned on Guru Nanak Dev ji that everything belonged to the ultimate Creator, to God.

Lao Tzu watched the wind blow a leaf lying on the ground into the sky and as the wind changed, the leaf started falling down. This was enough to awaken in Lao Tzu the realization that when something takes you to lofty heights, do not think that you have achieved it. When you start coming down, do not struggle to stay afloat, because that something is now not keeping you in that position.

No one can become God, but everybody has the potential to be empty so that God can descend. This is ultimate wellness.

Way to God

Humans fear the unknown, whether it is God or death. Be God loving and not God fearing to overcome this fear. Develop your heart centre because love is the only way to God. You cannot reach Him by running away from the world. Live in this world, love this world; only then you can feel the presence of God in every aspect of creation.

Feel Him first in yourself, only then you can feel Him in others. The Hindu salutation of *'namaskar'* is an expression of this understanding. In doing a *namaskar*, you fold your hands, place them in front of your heart, close your eyes, and silently bow down to the person in front to convey that the God in me is bowing to the God in you. Live this way to reach God.

This world is so beautiful. How beautiful must be its creator! In order to become one with Him, die the wellness death, because only then your soul returns to its source, God.

WELLNESS DEATH

Death defines life

Life completes its journey in death. People do not want to talk about death because they are afraid of it. Is the fear because of death or because of what will happen after death? Since nobody knows for sure what will happen after death then that cannot be the cause of fear. We fear death itself. The more a person advances in age, the more this fear grips him. Death cannot be conquered, but the fear of death can be. If the fear of death is overcome, all other fears will vanish. Wellness death is when you have no fear of death. It is the ultimate in human evolution. Art of self-wellness is not complete till you have mastered the art of dying.

What is Death?

Life is a delicate balance of Eros (instinct to live) and Thanatos (death instinct). Both are present in us all the time. When Thanatos overpowers Eros, life moves into death. There is irreversible severance of your physical body's relations with the world. Is death also the severance of your relations with your soul and mind? It is not. If you have been aware of your soul and mind, then you can accept this fact. In that case, there is no death.

The soul and mind do not die, but the physical body does. The visible part dies. The invisible part moves on. You are invisible before you enter your mother's womb; you become invisible again after death. Your soul may either enter another physical body or not return. Either way, there is no death.

Ram Naresh Tripathi, a Hindi poet says, 'Death is like a river in which the living being takes a dip to refresh itself and begins the journey of life afresh.' He hints at the continuum of life with a small prelude in death.

Buddha was asked where he will go after death. He replied that when an earthen pot breaks, the space contained in the pot merges with the space around it and the earth merges with earth. Similarly, the space contained in his body will merge with the space, and the body will return to earth from where it has come.

Socrates interpreted that death is either a state of nothingness and utter unconsciousness, or of migration of the soul from this world to the other. Unconsciousness gives profound bliss of a dreamless sleep, and the other world gives you an opportunity to once again meet your friends and foes. In both the cases, death is good and there is nothing evil in it.

According to Greek mythology, Hypnos (sleep) and Thanatos (death) are half-brothers. You move from the arms of Hypnos to Thanatos. You sleep and do not wake up. Sleep gives you a new day and death gives you a new life. We welcome sleep, but shun death because we go to sleep assured in our mind that we will wake up from sleep. However, we are not sure of our journey after death.

Death is not a sudden occurrence (except accidental death). In all other cases, the ability of the body to draw energy from the environment gradually diminishes in the last six months or one year of life. When it cannot draw sustenance, it dies. It is like falling of a leaf. When the leaf loses its capability to draw nutrition from the plant, then the nutrients of the leaf start returning to the plant. When all the nutrients have returned, the leaf falls. Animals recognize this instinctively, but the human intellect does not.

In the last 48 hours of her life, our dog, Czaro, had stopped taking food and water. We had made her comfortable in a secluded place near our bedroom. She was very feeble and could hardly move, but she was not in pain. At 4 o'clock in the morning, I was surprised to see that she had moved to her favourite carpet next to our bed and was lying their peacefully. Her rapid breathing indicated that she was in her last moments of life. She was conscious and responded to our touch and tried to raise her paw to shake hands. We sat next to her and patted her to reassure her of our love in her last moments. Suddenly her jaw relaxed. She stopped breathing. I could feel the pulsation of blood behind her ears. Few seconds later, it had stopped. Her soul had left the body. There was no cry of death. It was like falling of a leaf—gentle, silent and painless.

Is there a Purpose in Death?

As per Shakespeare, there is none because he says: 'Like flies to the wanton boys, Gods kill us for their daily sport.' But death has many purposes.

Death is for Recycling

Energy can neither be created nor destroyed. When the creation wants fresh matter, it destroys the old matter and converts it into energy from which new matter can be created. Death continues the cycle of creation.

Death is for Renewal

Alfred Tennyson said, 'Old order changeth yielding place to new.' Death gets rid of the old so that the new can come in. Death takes you out of the previous life so that you can start a new life.

Death is Therapeutic

It cures what you cannot endure. The next life again gives you a taste of bliss in the womb to give you another chance to achieve blissfulness and heal yourself.

Death is a Teacher

It teaches you that the body is not permanent. Do not get attached to it.

Death puts a Period on your Life

If there was no death, then we would have no constraints to do anything within a particular time. Just imagine the consequences. Walk out of the slavery of your mind, drop your ego and seek your soul within this limited time. This quest makes your life large within the same length. This is what the famous dialogue in the Hindi film '*Anand*' conveys: '*Zindagi lambi nahin, badi honi chahiye*', meaning that 'life should be large and not long.

Why Nobody Wants to Die?

Life is so enchanting that nobody wants to die. Even the worst sufferer wants to endure it and live. Existence is so intoxicating that even if it makes us suffer, we still want to live forever. History and literature are replete with anecdotes of humans who have attempted to prolong life as well as escape death.

Nobody wants to die because everyone is still not satisfied with the way one has lived. We want to live more, till we have satisfied our desires. Desires never get fulfilled. Our attachments, which shall be left behind and on which we will have no control, do not let us die. We do not want to lose or feel the absence, so we chase deathless living. However, if one gets detached, then it becomes easy to depart.

Despite seeing death all around, one maintains a feeling that it will not happen to me. This feeling is because the permanence of your soul is shining through your mind. The soul maintains this spark of immortality, because of which the thought of death does not grip us. We live in a sense of eternity and never think that life will end one day. Since we do not have any personal experience of our soul, we become sad when our dear and near ones die.

We do not want to die because of the fear of unknown. We want to go on living and avoid the unknown but ultimately the unknown beckons us. Mirza Ghalib said:

> 'Maut ka din muayyan hai,
> Neend kyon raat bhar nahin aati!'

'Death is preordained, why are you restless all the time!'

Art of Dying

Biologically death is built into us. This departure is the only certainty. The art of dying is to accept it and surrender, while there is time and depart peacefully and gracefully. The most ancient thought about the art of dying is in the Vedic prayer, 'May the years of life assigned to me be peaceful.' The prayer is neither for long life nor seeking deliverance from death.

Recognize the Declining Trend of your Prana

You can do it only if you have been reading your body and mind every day. You can either struggle to arrest it or accept it to prepare for death. In struggle you will make life painful for yourself and others around you. Accept it and wait patiently for the final moment. Ancient wisdom maintains that when the tip of the nose and ear lobes droop, the countdown for your death has stared.

Dying is an Individual Affair

You must die alone. Nobody can die for you or with you. All those who travelled with you in your life will not accompany you in death and beyond. Be grateful to them. Take leave of them. Drop all attachments. Let go. Finally, withdraw your attachments with your body and mind to a level that the body and mind become inconsequential. Then soul shines through and you can watch when it leaves the body. Also, you will not carry any baggage from previous life.

Witness the Passing Away of your Soul from the Body

Most people lose consciousness before they die. It is not due to the fear of death or the pain that death may cause. Death is painless. The consciousness is lost because we try to delay death and prolong life; it is this attempt to unnaturally prolong it that causes unbearable pain and makes the body unconscious. Since you are unconscious, you cannot witness your soul leaving the body. The opportunity to experience the greatest moment of life is thus lost.

If you have not been watchful all your life and not become aware of your soul, then you cannot watch your soul at the moment of death.

If you have been watchful in every moment, only then can you be watchful in the moment of death.

It is said that Socrates tried to watch his last moments. When he was given the cup of poison to drink, his followers started wailing. He asked them to keep quiet so that he could concentrate on the experience of his death. He told his disciples, 'I want to observe the transition of life into death. If the soul is still there when my body dies, then there is no reason for crying, because life is going to continue. If there is no soul when the body dies, there is no reason to cry even then, because all that I have done in this life is over forever.' The numbness, because of poison, affected his body gradually. He could not feel his feet and legs, but he was still alive. Gradually, he stopped feeling his arms and hands, but something in him was still alive. Eventually he could not feel his whole body, but his awareness did not leave him. When he came to the point where he could barely speak, he gave the last message, 'Crito, we owe a cock to Asclepius. Please do not forget to pay the debt.' His cryptic message conveyed that the soul, which is a custodian of all information, is alive and that it must not carry any unpaid debt in its journey ahead, and the soul survives death. So, one should not be afraid of death.

I[1] have watched three deaths from very close quarters. I was feeling my mother's pulse when she stopped breathing. Her pulse fluttered, paused and then the last beat of the heart gave a forceful pulse. Her soul left her body. When my father's heart stopped, the doctor was all prepared to give him a cardiac shock, but I stopped him because the soul was in the process of transition, and any violence to the body would have caused disturbance to his peaceful passing away. My father- in-law's heart suddenly stopped. By the time I could feel his pulse, he was gone.

Life is on the razor's edge. It ends in a moment. Since nobody knows when, it is better to be prepared for it. See yourself dead every day for a short period as a practice. Make your body still. Stop your mind. Feel that the soul is looking at you. It may give you a glimpse of this ultimate event of life.

Why Wellness Death?

Death decides your birth. As you die so you are born. It is like sleep. As you sleep so you wake up. If you sleep peacefully, you will wake up peaceful. If you die peacefully, you will be born peaceful. If you die knowingly, you will be born awakened.

Mourning

What happens beyond death is only a conjecture. Kirlian photography has captured that when a leaf is plucked, the

---

[1] S. B. Sehajpal

bioluminescence of the leaf continues in the space previously occupied by the leaf. As per Hindu philosophy, the soul continues to wander in the vicinity for 13 days and then goes to the new journey. You may feel the presence of the person for that many days. Probably it takes those many days for the memory in the brain to recede or may be the invisible part (mind and soul) lingers on for these many days!

The memory about your dear one, who has died, stays in your conscious mind. Memory about you, carried by the departed soul, goes into the unconscious mind of the new body in which that soul has entered. What you think about that dear one in your conscious mind reaches the unconscious mind of that person in their new birth through collective mind. It affects that person in new life. So mourn not the dead because that will cause them grief. Wish them well so that they feel good.

A NOTE TO THE READER

The mind makes man uneasy. As a result, the body becomes diseased, which in turn causes greater distress to the mind. This vicious cycle continues till death and then starts again after birth. Your mind makes you uneasy because it sees you different from others. Remove this ignorance because all are one. Due to evolution, humans are capable of becoming aware of their soul, mastering their mind and averting its mischief. The collective effort by mankind to awaken the soul has not produced the desired results on a large scale. Thus, individual effort is necessary to put humans at ease. If every human becomes peaceful, then mankind will become peaceful too.

Three lines sum up this book:

Light food.
Light mood.
Light exercise.

Devote two hours out of twenty-four to exercise, practise pranayama, bathe, eat and meditate. Follow the wellness way of life for a definite period to help improve your health and achieve a state of wellness. We suggest that you calculate one day per year of your life to define your test period. For instance, if you are 70 years of age, then give yourself at least 70 days to practise the wellness way of life.

Answer three questions to monitor your progress:

Have you self-actualized?
Have you self-realized?
Have you God-realized?

Since every aspect of wellness cannot be covered in one book, there may be many comments and clarifications which this book might invite. We shall be more than pleased to respond to the best of our ability. We encourage you to share your experiences to enrich our understanding of wellness. We shall be grateful.

Peace be on all

Lt General S. B. Sehajpal
sbsehajpal32@gmail.com

Mrs Kiran Sehajpal
kiransehajpal@rediffmail.com

READERS' REVIEWS

No more psychiatric medicines for me because the book has brought me out of the dark phase of my life.
Dr C.B. Sharma, Maxillofacial Surgeon

A riveting narrative, beautifully expressed to give insight into an entirely different way of living life.
Major General V. K. Sinha, VSM, Orthopedic Surgeon

Mythology, psychology, physiology and philosophy have been beautifully woven into the narrative.
Colonel Tashu Kakar

Excellent bedside book which must be read by everyone.
Dr Apar Bindra, Phd(France)

A well conceived and highly inspirational book to lead a healthy life.
Navneeta Taneja, Educationist

Billions of $$$ could not keep Steve Job alive. This book gives a simple solution to healthy body, mind and soul.
Colonel Gurdip Saund, Electronics Engineer

Loads of information to stay healthy by paying attention to bathing, sleeping, eating, etc. A must have in personal library.
Dr Shveta Gupta, Ophthalmologist

An encyclopedia of information on wellness.
Dr Kailash Mohan, Dental Surgeon

www.ingramcontent.com/pod-product-compliance
Lightning Source LLC
LaVergne TN
LVHW041706070526
838199LV00045B/1234